BEFORE
THE DREAM

BEFORE THE DREAM

MARTIN LUTHER KING'S 1963 SPEECH, AND CIVIL RIGHTS STRUGGLES IN FORT WAYNE, INDIANA

CHRISTOPHER ELLIOTT

America Through Time is an imprint of Fonthill Media LLC
www.through-time.com
office@through-time.com

Published by Arcadia Publishing by arrangement with Fonthill Media LLC
For all general information, please contact Arcadia Publishing:
Telephone: 843-853-2070
Fax: 843-853-0044
E-mail: sales@arcadiapublishing.com
For customer service and orders:
Toll-Free 1-888-313-2665

www.arcadiapublishing.com

First published 2021

Copyright © Christopher Elliott 2021

ISBN 978-1-63499-340-1

Typeset in 10.5pt on 13.5pt Sabon
Printed and bound in England

Foreword

I was beyond excited to learn of a new book about Dr. Martin Luther King. There has never been a question of Dr. King's greatness or that his legacy would live on long after his untimely demise. I was born and raised in Fort Wayne, Indiana, and have lived here for most of my life. Dr. King's visit in 1963 preceded my birth in 1965, but I remember hearing stories about that memorable event; my father, Pastor Samuel Walker, along with pastors and community leaders, were instrumental in making that event happen. It was a joy for my young colleagues and myself when we were in the tender years of our ministries as we sat and listened to the "old preachers, reminisce about that event and other local battels for our civil rights." I knew that Chris was on point when he mentioned the group of protestors at the event. I remember him and the other preachers saying, "Doc, they couldn't do nothing with ole King but kill him, could they."

As I consider our country's climate, I believe that race relations in America are worse today than they were in 1963. So much is hidden, even with Trump, the Proud Boys, and the millions of racists and white supremacists that suddenly emerged "out of the woodwork," as my mother would say. Yes, legal segregation was outlawed, and laws against discrimination changed; unfortunately, laws do not eradicate hate, bigotry, or ignorance. Despite the many advances made, I am convinced that racism in some form is present in every state, city, community, and neighborhood in this country. African Americans and other minorities daily suffer red-lining, unfair lending practices, and social injustice, to name a few offenses. It saddens me to make that statement today in early 2021. My heart breaks even more to live out that statement every day of my life as a black man in America.

In *Before the Dream*, Chris Elliott has provided an eloquent, accurate, and timely reminder that there is still much work to do for Dr. King's dream to be a reality. By providing a snapshot of Dr. King's life, Mr. Elliott also reminds those who would pursue racial equality of the high price tag attached to true freedom. This freedom is not just for us but for all those who will come after us. I pray daily for my children and grandchildren.

The day I can jog in a different neighborhood without suspicious looks from residents, and my wife can shop in Von Maur without being followed around by a clerk, we will have achieved a real America. When the police can stop my son for a traffic violation without being terrified that he might be killed by those who are supposed to protect him, then the work of Dr. King and all the others who have pursued equality will be completed. At that time, we will be "living the dream." Thank you, Chris, for reminding us of the work yet to be done.

Prophet Cedric L. Walker, Sr.
ProphetCedWalk Ministries

Acknowledgments

We always remember the first time: the first time we fell in love; the first time we rode a bike; the first time we played catch with our father; the first comforting hug from our mother; the first time we drove a car; the first time we tasted a food that we savored; the first time we were fearful. We also remember the first time we became totally absorbed with emotional inspiration.

I was fifteen years old the first time I became enthralled with Martin Luther King. I was watching a Bill Moyers television special with my father in 1983 commemorating the twentieth anniversary of the March on Washington. Dr. King was delivering his incomparable "I Have a Dream" speech. I was mesmerized. From that moment forward, I have been fascinated with the life of Dr. Martin Luther King and the Civil Rights movement. How fitting that the first time I endeavor to write and publish a book of historical nature, the subject matter pertains to an area of personal interest and passion.

Publishing a book fulfills a lifelong dream. This journey could not have been completed without the help of many individuals. First, I would like to thank local author Randy Harter for his advice as I launched my project, as well as generously sharing several connections pertinent to my research, including former Mayor Paul Helmke. Mr. Helmke then graciously shared his recollections of Dr. King's speech, and connected me with his good friends, Peter and Gregory Meister.

I would like to thank all of the following individuals who agreed to participate in a Zoom conference that I hosted during July 2020 to discuss the modern state of race relations in America: Marshall White, Bennie Edwards, Denise Porter-Ross, Darrion White, Jovan Barnes, Rev.

Cedric Walker, Jahrae Hampton, Khalid Griffin, and Joe Adams. The rich conversation lasted two hours and could have continued indefinitely. Thank you for donating your time to discuss this important topic, and for sharing your life experiences.

Thank you to my family for your support and encouragement, including my stepdaughters Ashley and Aubrey, stepson Taylor, and son Nathan. Thanks to my mother for your everlasting kindness and support. Also, a major shout-out to my brother-in-law Brian Sirois, who once again demonstrated his talents as a photographer with his stunning photos of the MLK bridge included in this book. I would like to extend a special thank you to my father for editing the first rough draft of my manuscript and advising me through the rewrite. A fresh set of objective eyes was necessary, and helpful. Finally, a special dose of gratitude for my wife Alicia. Thank you for your patience, support, and your unconditional love.

Contents

Introduction:
Before the Dream

I enjoy bike rides; they are a peaceful part of my exercise ritual. Frequently, I will venture into neighborhoods where I do not live. During these rides, I have never once experienced suspicious looks from residents as I traveled past their comfortable suburban homes. Instead, I often receive welcoming waves and pleasant smiles. Walking my dog after sunset in my own neighborhood provides me with tranquility at the conclusion of an active day. During these evening walks, never have I worried that a paranoid neighbor would call the police to investigate my activities. Never have I shopped in a retail store while a sales associate followed me closely under the assumption that I had criminal intentions. Never have I had reason to believe that I was denied employment or housing opportunities due to the color of my skin. Never have I been pulled over by law enforcement fearful of a police officer's anxious trigger finger. Never have I experienced agitated looks from older women clutching their purses tightly as I walked past them on the street. Never have I listened to rap music in my car and exchanged glances with nearby motorists who assume that I was a member of a criminal street gang. Never have I experienced fearful stares and immediate car alarm activation in parking lots while strolling past a customer's vehicle.

I have never been subjected to these experiences because I am a privileged white man. I have never personally experienced, therefore cannot possibly fully comprehend, life as an American black man.

Racial injustice has existed in America since its founding. Although some wounds have healed, many open sores remain. The scars of injustice have never disappeared. In our current political climate, blatant racism has become more vociferous and acceptable than we have witnessed in decades.

As a result, the amount of progress we have made toward racial unity and equal opportunity is teetering further away from Martin Luther King's dream of equality.

Arrested a total of thirty times during his quest for freedom, King was a 5-foot 7-inch intellectual giant of a man. He was a child prodigy who seemed destined for greatness at an early age. A high school graduate at the age of fifteen, a college graduate and ordained minister at the age of nineteen, he earned a Bachelor of Divinity degree aged twenty-two, and a PhD at twenty-six. Born and raised in Atlanta, Georgia, King dreamed of permanently blurring color lines to ensure unity and equal opportunity for all races during the Civil Rights movement of the 1950s and 1960s. His optimism for turning his dream into reality was evident during his Nobel Peace Prize acceptance speech in Oslo, Norway, December 10, 1964:

> I refuse to accept the view that mankind is so tragically bound to the starless midnight of racism and war that the bright daybreak of peace and brotherhood can never become a reality.... I believe that unarmed truth and unconditional love will have the final word.

King's aspirations for racial unity during the Civil Rights struggle often initiated a dichotomy of emotions in most Americans. Some found his optimism intoxicating and supported his progressively ambitious crusades. Others felt uncomfortable that their *status quo* and position of power was being threatened by the influential leadership of a persuasive, southern, black, Baptist minister. Resistance to that change was often voiced loudly. An example of this division occurred in June 1963 when Dr. King visited my hometown of Fort Wayne, Indiana, to lead a rally downtown at the Scottish Rite auditorium.

Dr. King visited during one of the most transformative and turbulent years in the Civil Rights movement. His speech, which was by most accounts a routine stop on his busy calendar, was sandwiched between two of the most impactful events during a year when a revolutionary spirit permeated both Fort Wayne, and the nation. In April 1963, only six weeks prior to his trip here, unrest and conflict in the segregated south landed Dr. King in a Birmingham, Alabama, jail for one week. King and Rev. Ralph Abernathy were arrested for peacefully protesting racial segregation. Part of his jail term was spent languishing in solitary confinement. Fire hoses and police dogs were used by the Birmingham police department to discourage and punish adolescent demonstrators. Thousands of children were jailed. Slightly over two months after his brief stay in Fort Wayne, Dr. King helped lead the March on Washington. This seminal event was held in the capitol mall next to the Lincoln Memorial, and was highlighted by King's unforgettable "I

Have a Dream" speech in front of an estimated crowd of 250,000 citizens.

Dr. King's 1963 Fort Wayne speech focused on the familiar refrain of social injustice toward African Americans throughout our country. He challenged the crowd to act swiftly to correct centuries of atrocities. Before a packed auditorium, in a mid-sized, Midwestern city, King urged its residents, of all races, to demand equality for all.

By all accounts, Dr. King's visit was relatively uneventful. No riots occurred. Fire hoses and police dogs were not used by law enforcement. A small crowd of white male segregationists peacefully protested outside the auditorium. No counter-protestors were present. There were no scuffles with police.

June 5, 1963 would prove to be Martin Luther King's only visit to Fort Wayne. The closest that he would venture here in the future was a speech that he gave on the campus of Manchester University, located forty-five minutes from the Fort Wayne on February 1, 1968—slightly more than two months before his death.

Dr. King possessed the ability to captivate and motivate like few men in the twentieth century. He founded, along with other black ministers, the Southern Christian Leadership Conference (SCLC), which was dedicated to implementing social change through non-violent means. Although his SCLC sponsored stop in Fort Wayne was routine, and represents only a sliver of the Civil Rights movement, the impact of that one visit on our city, and the State of Indiana, was extraordinary. Fifty-eight years later, his presence lingers. His speech still resonates with past and present city residents. It represents a significant highlight in our history. The Dr. Martin Luther King memorial bridge, completed in 2012, illuminates Fort Wayne evenings with stunning, multi-color LED lighting. The bridge crosses the St. Mary's River and stands proudly as a gateway into downtown. Recently our city-council approved a bill to provide Fort Wayne residents a permanent memorial of Dr. King's visit. As of this writing, city officials are considering how such a remembrance will be designed, and where it will be located.

King was an imperfect man with perfect elocution and perfect execution of a perfect vision. This city celebrates one powerful visit, by one incomparable man. Before the dream.

1

Life in 1963 Nationally— Parading Without a Permit

1963

It is 1963 in America. Life expectancy is a touch under the age of seventy; America's average annual income is $5,800; gas is 30 cents per gallon; John F. Kennedy is President of the United States; the U.S. Postal Service has introduced the zip code; smoking is considered reasonably safe; automobile seatbelts are optional; few women work outside the home; segregation laws are being challenged; and Communism threatens our freedom.

During the Cuban Missile Crisis in October 1962, the U.S. and Soviet Union pushed catastrophically close to nuclear war after Soviet nuclear facilities were spotted in Cuba by American intelligence. The escalating threat of Communism infiltrating our nation consumed our leaders after narrowly avoiding a global cataclysm. Citizens suspected of being communist sympathizers are shadowed by multiple branches of law enforcement, including the FBI. One such citizen was Dr. Martin Luther King. Two close associates of King were accused of siding with Communism, leading the FBI to closely monitor King's activities.

King developed an interest in Communism while a student at Crozer Theological Seminary during the late 1940s. Although King disagreed with the more aggressive fundamental principles that guide Communist philosophy, doctrine proposing methods for the elimination of poverty and narrowing of the income gap piqued his interest. While courting Coretta Scott, King once declared in a letter to his future wife that he was "more socialistic in my economic theory that capitalistic."

During King's rise to national fame following the success of the Montgomery

Bus Boycott in 1955–56, friendships developed with several salient citizens who possessed ties to the Communist party. These friendships included prominent New York Jewish attorney Stanley Levinson, who would become one of Dr. King's closest advisers throughout the Civil Rights movement. Despite rendering a multitude of essential services, including the preparation of King's tax returns, raising money for the SCLC, and helping to edit some of King's books and speeches, Levinson refused compensation.

Levinson was known to the FBI as a member, and major financial contributor, of the Communist Party USA (CPUSA). FBI Chief J. Edgar Hoover believed wholeheartedly that the Civil Rights movement was part of a Communist plot to destroy America via racial uprising. Sparking alarm within the FBI community was Levinson's influence on King, convincing Hoover that both were a threat to national security.

In addition to Levinson, King had also formed a partnership with successful businessman Jack O'Dell. After hearing King speak at Dexter Avenue Baptist Church in Montgomery, Alabama, during the mid-1950s, O'Dell became inspired to join the Civil Rights cause. He helped to organize fundraising activities for the SCLC and participated in marches for integration. Like Levinson, O'Dell was on the FBI's radar as a member of the CPUSA. Both men were under FBI surveillance.

By February 1962, Hoover relayed his concerns about King's associates to President John F. Kennedy and his administration. Hoover requested wiretap authorization. Hopeful for a diplomatic resolution, the request for surveillance on Dr. King was denied by Attorney General Robert Kennedy. More than one year later, the Kennedy's met with King privately on June 22, 1963. After discussing plans for the March on Washington with King and other Civil Rights leaders, the Kennedy's requested a private meeting with King, at which time they expressed their concerns about his relationships with Levinson, and O'Dell.

The president demanded that King terminate relationships with both men. For the good of the movement, King and O'Dell reluctantly bowed to pressure, and complied with the Kennedy's request to sever their professional relationship. In his resignation letter to King, O'Dell called his work with the SCLC "a rewarding experience which I shall always cherish." King continued, however, to work closely with Levinson.

By late 1963, after it became evident that King had maintained his association with Levinson, Hoover finally persuaded the Kennedy administration to authorize wiretaps. King's Atlanta home, office, and telephones were wired with listening devices, in addition to hotel rooms where he would stay while traveling. Through wiretaps placed in hotel rooms, the FBI learned that King was engaged in several extramarital affairs. The agency used this sensitive information in future attempts to strong-arm

King into compliance, including one instance where he was encouraged to commit suicide to prevent public shame. These bureau tactics proved to be unsuccessful.

Birmingham

The threat of Communism and the quest for Civil Rights dominated both the print and electronic news cycles during this era. Perhaps no year during the struggle for Civil Rights and racial equality was stormier, or more pivotal, than 1963. Unrest in heavily segregated Birmingham, Alabama, during the spring of 1963 would captivate the nation. Overcoming terrorism from the Ku Klux Klan, police brutality, a racist power structure and an overwhelmingly prejudiced local citizenry represented a monumental challenge for the Civil Rights movement in a city notoriously referred to as "Bombingham."

Reverend Fred Shuttlesworth had been leading the Civil Rights crusade in Birmingham for nearly a decade. In 1956, the KKK bombed Shuttlesworth's home with sixteen sticks of dynamite following his efforts to desegregate the city. Although the Shuttlesworth family was home at the time, and his home destroyed, everybody escaped with only minor injuries. In 1957, he was beaten with chains and baseball bats, and his wife was stabbed after both attempted to enroll their daughter at an all-white high school. Rev. Shuttlesworth also participated in the 1961 Freedom Rides. Despite Shuttlesworth's heroic efforts, minimal progress was achieved.

King, Ralph Abernathy, and other leaders within the Southern Christian Leadership Conference (SCLC) descended on Birmingham, and merged with the local Alabama Christian Movement for Christian Rights (ACMHR), an organization founded by Rev. Shuttlesworth, to hatch "Project C," for confrontation. Direct, but peaceful confrontation was to be deployed to address and destroy generations of Birmingham bigotry.

Typical of most segregation in the south, black and white Birmingham citizens were forbidden from sitting together in movies theaters and restaurants. "Whites only" signs hung on doorways and water fountains throughout the city. Segregation in Birmingham proved to be grotesquely inhumane.

Black citizens were not allowed to try on clothes at department stores. Black citizens had to guess their clothing size, and hope they fit correctly. They were not allowed to try on shoes. Many black Birmingham citizens would trace an outline of their feet on cardboard at home, bring the cutout with them to city shoe stores, then hold the board against the bottom of shoe soles looking for the right fit. Only white citizens were allowed to use conventional elevators. The back elevators were reserved for "niggers and freight." Residential listings in the city telephone book would indicate "C" for colored. Black-owned businesses were also noted with the "C" distinction in the yellow pages.

Taking road trips throughout Alabama, and much of the south, presented additional challenges. Since there were few opportunities for blacks to find a restaurant that would serve them, most black families would pack picnic lunches. Meals often had to be eaten inside automobiles since many parks were also segregated or banned their presence altogether. Most gas stations would not allow blacks to use their bathroom facilities, causing black citizens to position themselves strategically for modest privacy and urinate or defecate behind their own car. Buckets and portable toilets were often carried in their car trunks. Few motels would allow them to rent a room for overnight lodging.

King and other Civil Rights activists sought to crumble the Birmingham hierarchy, and forever halt future generations of racial discrimination. The majority of the campaign called for boycotts of downtown businesses during Easter weekend—traditionally one of the busiest shopping weekends of the year. During the Montgomery Bus Boycott of 1955–56, King experienced firsthand how economic impact can equate to social impact. This same philosophy was to be deployed in Birmingham.

Public Safety Commissioner and recent Mayoral candidate Bull Connor fervently vowed to maintain the *status quo* at all costs. In an effort to prevent a mass demonstration, King, Ralph Abernathy, Shuttlesworth, and the rest of the SCLD and ACMHR leadership were given a court order preventing "boycotting, trespassing, parading, picketing, sit-ins, kneel-ins, wade-ins, and inciting or encouraging such acts." On Good Friday, April 12, 1963, King and Abernathy decided to defy the court order with a downtown march. They were arrested, and held in Birmingham jail, separately, in solitary confinement, for their first twenty-four hours. "You will never know the meaning of utter darkness until you have lain in such dungeon, knowing that sunlight is streaming overhead and seeing only darkness below," King recalled from his prison experience. King and Abernathy were denied the opportunity to place any telephone calls, including their lawyers. President John F. Kennedy intervened and successfully convinced the Birmingham police department to provide more suitable arrangements. The president also placed a calming phone call to Coretta Scott King to offer his support. Following President Kennedy's intervention, King and Abernathy were visited by attorneys, Arthur Shores, and Orzell Billingsley. King was also visited by friend and attorney Clarence Jones, who informed Dr. King that actor and singer Harry Belafonte had successfully raised $50,000 in bail money. King exclaimed that the news "lifted a thousand pounds from my heart."

King and Abernathy were detained in Birmingham jail for over one week.

During their confinement, Dr. King composed an appeal to several local members of the clergy who had criticized the actions, and timing, of King and the other Civil Rights activists. Composed primarily on scraps of paper, and in the margins of a newspaper, King's essay would become the literary masterpiece "Letter from a Birmingham Jail," one of the most influential publications to develop from the Civil Rights movement. "Injustice anywhere is a threat to justice everywhere," one of King's most poignant quotes, was born from this letter. The letter was not released for public consumption for over two months.

King and Abernathy were released from jail one week later, on April 20, 1963. Their bail of $160,000 was paid by a local UAW official. Upon their release, plans were then developed for what became known as the children's crusade. This next step in the Birmingham campaign called for the inclusion of children, some elementary school aged, to participate in demonstrations. Despite the risk of serious physical injury, and mental distress to young children, black families were convinced by King and others that a likely barbaric response from the Birmingham police department would generate national news and could merge public opinion in their favor. Recent demonstrations in Albany, Georgia, failed to bring shock value. They were peaceful, and devoid of significant police misconduct. Segregationist Birmingham Police commissioner Bull Connor, on the other hand, had a hot tempered and bigoted reputation. The opportunity for physical conflict was much greater. SCLC leaders hoped that Connor and the police force could be trapped into confrontation, leading to visuals that might convince much of white America to become involved in the push for desegregation, and decency toward all citizens, regardless of race. The plan succeeded.

Downtown demonstrations began with hundreds of local black children. Connor ordered the use of attacking police dogs and fire hoses to disrupt and discourage the demonstrations. Water pressure from fire hoses was powerful enough to strip bark from trees. Children, some under the age of ten, and young adults, suffered contusions and broken bones once blasted with water. Reverend Shuttlesworth was nearly killed after water blasts caused him to stumble down the front steps of his church. After learning that Rev. Shuttlesworth was injured by the fire hose blasts, Bull Connor remarked to *The New York Times*: "I'm sorry I missed it. I wish they'd carried him away in a hearse."

Images of terrorized child protestors were published in newspapers around the world. Violent video opened the evening news and disrupted regular programming. Thousands were locked in crowded jail cells. Much of America, and the world, was outraged.

Following several days of peaceful demonstrations provoking violent police responses, Dr. King called for a truce on May 8, 1963 to negotiate with Birmingham city officials. Two days later, King led a press conference to proudly announce that an agreement had been reached. Within ninety days, city leaders agreed to desegregate restaurants and drinking fountains, in addition to providing more suitable employment opportunities. The following day, May 11, 1963, King returned home to Atlanta. He barely escaped death.

During their involvement in the Birmingham campaign, King, Abernathy, and other SCLC officials stayed in the prestigious A. G. Gaston motel. Gaston, a successful local black businessman, owned and operated the minority friendly hotel and restaurant, in addition to several other area enterprises. Just before midnight, May 11, 1963, several sticks of dynamite were thrown by local KKK members toward Room 30—King's room—at the Gaston motel. Room 30, and others nearby, were obliterated. After receiving the news, King remarked the following day that the dynamite "was placed as to kill or seriously wound anyone who might have been in Room 30—my room. Evidently the would-be assassins did not know I was in Atlanta that night." The home of A. D. King, Dr. King's younger brother, was bombed that same evening. The front wall of his home was destroyed. The bomb also left a 4-foot by 5-foot gaping hole in his yard. Amazingly, A. D. King was not injured, even though his family was home sleeping at the time. "It's a brick," said the younger King, describing the material construction of his home. "That's the only thing that saved us."

The coordinated bombings deliberately occurred as bars were closing for the evening in predominantly black sections of town. Simmering anger and frustration boiled over that evening as riots erupted in the streets of Birmingham's black neighborhoods. Thousands of protestors tangled with law enforcement. Fires were started. Cars were overturned. Billy clubs cracking against black citizens' skulls could be heard from nearby witnesses while the crowd chanted "They started it!"

Dr. King later remarked that he suspected the bombs were set in hopes of provoking a riot. A. D. King arrived at the scene pleading with protestors to silence the violence. His request was ignored. Birmingham Mayor Albert Boutwell ordered the use of Alabama state troopers, many of whom remained in town for the children's crusade, to restore order. "The nigger King ought to be investigated by the Attorney General and the White House," the mayor remarked. "I hope every drop of blood that's spilled, he tastes in his throat, and I hope he chokes on it."

Following the conclusion of the Birmingham campaign, on May 24, 1963, Bobby Kennedy arranged for a meeting with several black activists at a residence he owned in New York City to discuss the tense state of race relations in America. Prominent black authors James Baldwin and Lorraine Hansberry, and singer Henry Belafonte were among those in attendance.

Kennedy and Baldwin had met during a White House dinner the previous year honoring winners of the Nobel Peace prize, of which Baldwin was a recipient.

Despite the assumption of good intentions, a disconnect and misunderstanding between white and black experiences became evident early, leading to an acrimonious meeting. The attorney general used the occasion of the meeting to promote claims of a stellar record on Civil Rights for their administration. His guests strongly disagreed. Jerome Smith, a black Civil Rights activist from Mississippi who had recently been physically assaulted by police and jailed during recent protests, grew agitated. After recounting the horror that he endured, Smith began weeping. The meeting became increasingly intense. Baldwin, Hansberry, and others in attendance grew increasingly frustrated with Kennedy, and his associates. Said Hansberry: "You have a great many very accomplished people in this room, Mr. Attorney General, but the only man you should be listening to is that man [Jerome Smith] over there. That is the voice of twenty-two million people." Voices were raised, and tempers continued to flare until Baldwin and Hansberry abruptly ended the meeting, storming out of Kennedy's apartment. By the summer of 1963, these events highlighted a fever pitch of contention in American race relations. However, the contentious meeting soon emboldened the Kennedy's attitudes toward Civil Rights, and the push for racial equality.

2

Life in Fort Wayne 1963: "The Mississippi of the North"

Fort Wayne: A Brief History

Fort Wayne, Indiana. Where we drink pop, not soda. We clean our house with a sweeper, not a vacuum cleaner. Indiana's second largest city is located at the confluence of three rivers: the St. Mary's, St. Joseph, and Maumee nestled in the Northeast corner of Indiana, a half-hour drive from the Ohio state line, and a forty-minute drive from Michigan. With a steadily growing population totaling approximately 270,000 people, the nation's seventy-ninth largest city takes its name from "Mad" Anthony Wayne, a hot-tempered eighteenth-century U.S. military general who established a fort near the area's rivers shortly after America secured victory in the Revolutionary War. Our city is often referred to by locals simply as "The Fort," or the "Summit City." When the Wabash-Erie canal extended through the area during the 1800s, it was discovered that Fort Wayne was the highest elevated city above sea level along the route, christening Fort Wayne with the Summit City nickname.

Extreme weather during any season in the Fort is not uncommon. Bone chilling winters with sub-zero wind chills lasting well into February, rainy Pacific Northwest-style springs with the threat of tornados, plus humid summers with temperatures reaching well into the 90s are all typical. The running joke in the area is that if you do not like the weather, just wait an hour, and it will change.

Traveling to dozens of area lakes over the summer is a popular pastime among many residents in the region. Informing your employer, family, or friends that you plan to spend the weekend at "the lake," without specifying which lake, is common to our regional vernacular.

Geographically, Fort Wayne is centrally located near several massive Midwestern, Great Lake-area cities that consistently rank near the top of most populated metropolitan areas in the nation. Drive three hours northeast, and you will find Detroit, plus the Canadian border. Four hours due east meanders along Lake Erie and lands you in Cleveland. Slightly over three hours southeast takes you to Cincinnati. Travel two hours southwest on I-69, and your destination becomes the state's capital city of Indianapolis. Drive four hours due west, and you will arrive in Chicago.

Numerous celebrities claim Fort Wayne in their roots. Scientist Philo T. Farnsworth, the inventor of the modern television, lived in the Fort for twenty years. Actress Carole Lombard, star of popular comedic films such as *My Man Godfrey, Nothing Sacred,* and *Mr. and Mrs. Smith,* was raised in the Fort as a child. Lombard later married Hollywood superstar Clark Gable. She died in a plane crash in 1942. A bridge located near her Fort Wayne childhood home is named in her honor. Emmy award winning actress Shelly Long, star of the immensely popular '80s sitcom *Cheers* hails from Fort Wayne. Long also starred in several films during the 1980s and 1990s. She is a graduate of South Side High School. Actor Dick York of *Bewitched* fame grew up in the city. World famous fashion designer Bill Blass was born and raised in Fort Wayne before moving to New York at the age of seventeen to attend Parson Design School. Blass would eventually launch a highly successful line of clothing, luggage, furs, and perfume that would bear his name, grossing hundreds of millions in sales every year. Suspense novelist Stephen King, author of best sellers such as *Christine, The Shining, Misery,* and *Cujo,* briefly lived in Fort Wayne as a child. Award-winning playwright and screenwriter Neil LaBute lived and worked in the city as an adult for a number of years. His first film, *In the Company of Men,* was shot on location in Fort Wayne during the mid-1990s. Popular actress and singer Heather Headley was born in Trinidad but moved to Fort Wayne as a teenager where she lived for several years. Dave Thomas, founder of the popular Wendy's fast-food restaurant chain, resided for years in Fort Wayne. His first food service job at Fort Wayne's Hobby House restaurant sparked his interest in food service entrepreneurship. Pulitzer Prize-winning *New York Times* journalist Charles Savage was born and raised here. Publisher William Rockhill Nelson, founder of the *Kansas City Star,* grew up in the Fort. Dr. Leonard Scheele, our nation's seventh surgeon general, appointed by President Harry S. Truman, was born, and raised in Fort Wayne. Popular '80s Christian rock band Petra has their roots in the city. Formidable Miami Indian chief Little Turtle lived in several areas in Fort Wayne and the surrounding area during the late 1700s and early 1800s until his death in 1812. Native American historians revere Little Turtle for both his military acumen and diplomatic abilities. Finally, one of Fort Wayne's most beloved residents lived in Fort Wayne during the mid-1800s. John Chapman, a missionary more commonly known as Johnny Appleseed, traveled the Midwest planting apple trees. Known for his generosity, devotion to conservation, and love of children, Chapman was admired everywhere he traveled. He died March 18, 1845. He is buried across a parking lot from the Memorial Coliseum. A nearby park is named in his honor. The annual Johnny Appleseed festival is held in the park every September and is one of the more popular events in the area.

Sports icons from the Fort have been plentiful. Popular '60s and '70s sportscaster Chris Schenkel resided here. Former basketball star Eugene Parker launched a sports agency empire representing primarily NFL football stars. Multiple NFL players were born and raised in Fort Wayne, including Anthony Spencer, Tyler Eifert, Vaughn Dunbar, Jaylon Smith, Rod Smith, Drue Tranquill, Bernard Pollard, Johnny Bright, Jason Baker, Trai Essex, James Hardy, Jesse Bates, Austin Mack, and Jason Fabini, in addition to NFL Hall of Famer and Super Bowl champion Rod Woodson. The city has produced professional baseball talents in Jarrod Parker, successful Major League baseball manager Eric Wedge, and Gold Glove winning outfielder Kevin Kiermaier. In basketball, 2015 Indiana Mr. Basketball winner Caleb Swanigan recently played in the NBA, while 2010 Mr. Basketball Deshaun Thomas has played professionally in Europe for nearly a decade. Walter Jordan starred for Northrop High School's 1974 state championship basketball team, then enjoyed a prolific college career at Purdue. Following a brief stint in the NBA, and several professional seasons in Europe, Jordan returned to Fort Wayne where for over a decade, he hosted a popular charity basketball event featuring a multitude of primarily Big-10 talent. Golfer Bill Kratzert, a four-time winner on the PGA tour during the 1970s and 1980s, grew up in Fort Wayne along with his LPGA sister Cathy Kratzert. Hockey players Dale Purinton and Fred Knipscheer spent brief periods in the NHL and called Fort Wayne home. Additionally, the city has produced Olympians such as Sharon Wichman, Matt Vogel, and Steve Bigelow in swimming, DeDee Nathan in Track & Field, Demarcus Beasley in soccer, and Lloy Ball in volleyball.

Minor league sports have a storied history in the city as well. The Fort Wayne Komets have forged an unmistakable entertainment and cultural identity that generations of fans have enjoyed since the 1950s. Eight championship banners spanning five different decades fly from the rafters of the Memorial Coliseum signifying a history of consistent success and fan loyalty that rivals any minor league hockey franchise in North America.

Class A minor league baseball arrived in 1993 with the Fort Wayne Wizards. Games were played at the newly built Memorial Stadium, located across the parking lot from the Memorial Coliseum, and adjacent to Johnny Appleseed park on the north side of town. At the time, they were an affiliate of the Minnesota Twins. The franchise switched affiliations to the San Diego Padres in the mid-2000s, a partnership that continues to this day. The Wizards were repackaged as the Tin Caps and moved downtown into newly built Parkview Field in 2009. The franchise won a Midwest League championship during that inaugural season. The Tin Caps award winning, state of the art minor league stadium with major league accommodations and aesthetics, became the jewel of downtown Fort Wayne. It has spurred unprecedented economic growth. Tin Caps attendance commonly ranks among the highest in the Midwest League, and throughout all minor league baseball.

Minor league basketball also resides in Fort Wayne. The Mad Ants, an NBA G-league franchise, and affiliate of the Indiana Pacers, launched in 2007. The Ants won a league championship in 2014.
Professional basketball once made its home in Fort Wayne. A team was founded in the early 1940s by local entrepreneur and basketball fan Fred Zollner, owner of a successful local foundry that manufactured automotive pistons. The Fort Wayne Pistons enjoyed loyal fan support until the mid-1950s, playing the majority of their home games at the Memorial Coliseum. In order to attract a larger audience, Zollner decided to relocate his franchise to Detroit following 1956–57 season. The Detroit Pistons have continued to thrive in the Motor City ever since that move, winning NBA titles in 1989, 1990, and 2004.

The city also has a proud baseball tradition that long predates the Tin Caps and Wizards. Some of our national pastime's earliest history can be traced to Fort Wayne. During the early days of Reconstruction following the Civil War, Fort Wayne's Kekionga Club shutout out the Forest City Club of Cleveland 2-0 on May 4, 1871 in the first ever documented professional baseball game. A monument was recently built and dedicated to commemorating the location of this historic occasion.

From 1907–1949, the Fort Wayne Colored Giants were one of the premier Negro league teams in the Midwest. The team disbanded two years after Jackie Robinson broke the color barrier in the Major Leagues. Games were played on several different fields around the city, including Lincoln Life field. Most games were played against other prominent black teams dotting the Midwest, such as the Toledo Mud Hens, Chicago Giants, Indianapolis ABC's, St. Louis Stars, Evansville White Sox, and the Pittsburgh Homestead Grays. The Colored Giants also routinely traveled to play all-white minor league teams in surrounding small cities, such as Decatur, Columbia City, LaGrange, and North Manchester, in addition to venturing across the state line to play all-white teams in Hicksville, Convoy, and Antwerp, Ohio. Although baseball was segregated, local communities often came together, both black and white, to cheer on their respective teams.

Ladies baseball also has a proud tradition in Fort Wayne. The All-American Girls professional baseball League (AAGPBL) initially founded during the World War II era by Phillip Wrigley, placed a franchise in the Summit City. The Fort Wayne Daisies were warmly received, and routinely drew large crowds to their games from 1945–1954. Games were initially played at North Side High School before switching to Memorial Park. Although the Daisies made the playoffs every year from 1947–1954, they failed to win an AAGPBL championship. The league disbanded following the end of the 1954 season. The popular 1992 movie *A League of their Own*, starring Tom Hanks, Geena Davis, and Rosie O'Donnell, is loosely based on the AAGPBL.

Fort Wayne is a city that registers only a blip of the Civil Rights movement radar. That lack of recognition is unfortunate. Similar experiences and events that advanced the movement in the south, and in America's largest cities, also impacted Fort Wayne and the surrounding region. This understated Midwest city of one-quarter million people has contributed significantly to the struggle for Civil Rights, and racial equality.

1963 Fort Wayne

It is June 1963. *Dr. No*, starring Sean Connery as the irrepressible James Bond, is the number one movie in America. You can catch the film's matinee at Fort Wayne's Clyde theater for a mere 85 cents. *It's my Party* by Lesley Gore is the number one hit song in the country. *The Beverly Hillbillies* is the most popular television show in the nation. Minimum wage is $1.25 per hour. A $5 bill comfortably buys you a box of Cheerios, a gallon of milk, and a loaf of bread from any grocery store in town with plenty of change leftover.

Paul Burns is mayor. Two months earlier, the city celebrated the Fort Wayne Komets first championship after defeating the Minneapolis Millers for the International Hockey League's Turner Cup. General Electric, Dana, and International Harvester sit among some of the rust belt city's largest employers. The discrepancy between white and black employment at these large industrial companies is glaring, and a cause for concern among area Civil Rights advocates.

Like many larger Midwestern cities during most of the twentieth century, Fort Wayne was part of the rust belt that served as the manufacturing base of the world. It was possible for many citizens to land a job at a factory with no formal education beyond high school, and work at the same manual labor, unionized job until retirement while earning a comfortable middle-class income. Most of the city's black families, however, did not enjoy this comfort.

Approximately 30,000 people worked at Fort Wayne's largest fourteen manufacturing companies in 1963. Only 3 percent of those workers were black. Unemployment in the city is three times higher for blacks than whites. Average income for whites nearly doubles average black income. Housing discrimination is common. As a result of the city's history of racial discrimination, Fort Wayne has notoriously earned the title, according to some members of the clergy, as the "Mississippi of the North." Fort Wayne Urban League Executive Secretary Robert Wilkerson declared "There must be a turning point" during a speech to local business leaders at the Hotel Van Orman on May 23, 1963. "We are in the midst of another emancipation, such as that proclaimed 100 years ago. The negro is determined to get all his rights now. He wants first class citizenship. He cannot be patient any longer. Don't say Birmingham can't happen here." Wilkerson's sense of urgency echoed those same pleas frequently uttered by Dr. Martin Luther King, and other Civil Rights leaders.

Wilkerson, a graduate of both Fisk University and the University of Minnesota, moved from Anderson, Indiana, to Fort Wayne in 1946. He was appointed executive secretary of the Fort Wayne Urban League the following year, a position that he would hold until 1967. Throughout his tenure, Wilkerson served as an outspoken and invaluable advocate for the city's black residents, challenging city government officials to promote equal opportunity for all.

According to U.S. census data, blacks comprised 7.2 percent of Fort Wayne's population in 1960. Prominent retail stores such as Sears and Wolf & Dessauer had only recently begun to hire their first black salesclerks. The freeway of progress toward racial equality was paved in Fort Wayne only to be impeded by road hazards. This frustrated not only Wilkerson, but other significant black leaders in town, such as Reverend Clyde Adams.

Spanning several decades of spiritual leadership, few religious leaders have impacted Fort Wayne communities more substantially than Reverend Adams. After graduating from East Night High School in Cincinnati, Adams enrolled at the University of Cincinnati where religion would become his primary focus and his life's work. The son of a sharecropper, Adams desired a higher quality of life. The church called Adams at a young age. He was accepted into the Michigan Baptist and Theological Seminary and School of Religion in Detroit where he would earn his degree in 1945.

While a student, Adams would meet his future wife Cordia Jones in Middletown, Ohio. "I was told they met at a public swimming pool," recalled his eldest son Joseph Adams. "Mom was sunbathing. It was love at first sight." They married in 1939, a union that would last more than sixty years until Cordia's passing in 2000. In addition to Joseph, the marriage produced three additional children: daughters Gloria and Karen, along with another son, John.

Reverend Adams initially led churches in both Addyston and Toledo, Ohio. Following those stints, he was called to lead Union Baptist in Fort Wayne in 1950, a church that already boasted a proud history in the black community.

Reverend Pius Barbour led what was then known as Mt. Olive Baptist Church in downtown Fort Wayne from 1931–33. Rev. Barbour had developed a friendship with Martin Luther King Sr. through their mutual affiliation with the National Baptist Association. While later teaching at Crozer Theological Seminary during the late 1940s, Rev. Barbour began mentoring Martin Luther King Jr. The two were known to challenge each other in spirited political debate. Dr. King considered Rev. Barbour one of his most influential mentors. They continued their friendship until Dr. King's death in 1968. During his rise to national and global prominence, Rev. Barbour once told young Dr. King: "Why God selected you, I don't know. All I know is that he has, and you are in a dangerous place."

From 1945–50, Rev. Phale Hale led Mt. Olive before accepting a new position with Union Grove Baptist Church in Columbus, Ohio. Rev. Hale became a classmate, and friend, of Martin Luther King while attending Moorehouse College in Atlanta, and stayed in touch with the Civil Rights icon for the remainder of Dr. King's life. On two occasions, King accepted Rev. Hale's invitation to speak at Union Grove during visits to Columbus and spent the night at his house.

While a Fort Wayne resident, Rev. Hale procured the help of several families from his congregation to assist in successfully integrating a downtown drugstore lunch counter. He also founded the city's chapter of the NAACP. Reverend Hale would continue his Civil Rights social activism after moving to Columbus and was also elected to seven consecutive terms in the Ohio House of Representatives before retiring from politics in 1980.

Shortly after his arrival, Reverend Adams oversaw the construction of a new building for Union Baptist Church on Smith Street in the Southeastern sector of Fort Wayne, a church that he would guide for over fifty years. To help fund the cost of building their new house of worship, Rev. Adams secured a $70,000 loan from a local bank. Union Baptist, under Rev. Adams leadership, became the city's first black church that was approved for financing from a local lending institution. In addition to guiding a faithful congregation, Reverend Adams became instrumental in influencing social change in the Summit City, leaving a legacy matched or exceeded by precious few Fort Wayne citizens.

Rev. Adams would serve as president of the Fort Wayne chapter of the NAACP for most of the 1950s. During this time, Rev. Adams would help lead the charge to desegregate Fort Wayne hotels, movie theaters, banks, hospitals, and restaurants. Furthermore, Rev. Adams also later joined

Rev. Jesse White and other area Civil Rights leaders in a successful boycott that fully integrated Fort Wayne Community Schools, the largest school system in the state of Indiana.

In addition to his local influence, Reverend Adams also left his mark with members of the National Baptist clergy. Adams taught a minister's tithing class, plus served on the board of directors for the National Baptist Convention for more than ten years. It was during this time that Reverend Adams would first meet and then develop a friendship with Rev. Martin Luther King. As their friendship blossomed, Adams, King, and other religious leaders would later collaborate to affect social change in the Fort Wayne area, and nudge the city closer to racial equality. These changes, however, were met with plenty of resistance similar to the rest of the nation.

Although "colored only" signs on drinking fountains or waiting areas were not to be found in Fort Wayne, black residents were nevertheless faced with daily doses of more subtle discrimination. Numerous city businesses refused to serve blacks. Redlining was common. It was understood that black residents were not permitted to apply for loans at certain banks. Nearly all black children in the city attended an aging Central High School while most white kids attended the more modern North and South Side High Schools. Only an occasional middle- to upper-class black child of a respected, local black professional attended either North or South Side high school with area white children. "We didn't have any black students at North Side until my senior year [in 1966]," recalled former Mayor Paul Helmke. A black police officer was a rarity. Rarer still were black political leaders or black school board members. Throughout post-World War II Fort Wayne, progress toward equal opportunity moved at a slow, methodical pace. "It was a difficult time," the late Reverend James Bledsoe of St. Johns Missionary Baptist Church reflected during a 1999 interview in the *Journal-Gazette*, "but we made the best of a bad situation."

Indicative of northern Indiana's resistance to full racial equality and representation was an invitation that the Fort Wayne Rotary Club extended to segregationist Mississippi governor Ross Barnett to speak at a Chamber of Commerce luncheon March 18, 1963. Barnett openly supported state's rights and the continuation of Jim Crow laws. He viciously opposed integration. Barnett once claimed that "the good Lord was the original segregationist…. He made us white because he wanted us white, and we intended that we should stay that way." During his visit to the Fort, Barnett shared this view of the Civil Rights movement with city Rotarians: "Plain old common sense should tell all right thinking Americans that this all-consuming interest in the so called civil rights of minority groups, by the politicians in Washington, is nothing in this world but dirty politics at its lowest level in the 187 years of this nation's history." Continuing, Barnett pleaded with his audience "to refuse to be brainwashed by those so-called liberals who are dedicated to the destruction of constitutional government in this nation under the false cry of civil rights."

While Barnett delivered his address, two multi-racial groups of protestors picketed his appearance outside the Chamber of Commerce building. One group was led by local NAACP President, and city dentist, Dr. Bernard Stuart. Seminarian Robert O'Sullivan led a group of predominantly white students who protested black living conditions in both the north and south.

Ongoing battles over desegregation, and a slew of other racial inequalities, plus Governor Barnett's invitation to speak, was a clear sign to area Civil Rights advocates that a bitter racial divide still existed in Fort Wayne. The same battles were being waged in the Summit City that were also being waged in the South, and across the nation. The Civil Rights movement in Fort Wayne needed the same boost as the rest of America.

3

Inviting Dr. King to the Fort

Racism, poverty, segregated seating in restaurants and movie theaters, gerrymandering, employment discrimination, housing discrimination, inadequate educational opportunities—like much of the nation, minorities were continually treated as second-class citizens in Fort Wayne. Influential members of the local clergy, and some political leaders, felt the time was right to invite Martin Luther King to the city to directly confront these concerns. Since he already had an established relationship with Dr. King, Reverend Adams would spearhead the process of arranging for the visit.

"Martin and I worked in the Department of Christian Education of the National Baptist Convention USA," recalled Adams in a January 2000 *News-Sentinel* article written by staff reporter Kevin Kilbane. "I had known him for several years." Ideally, the SCLC-King rally would be held at Union Baptist, or another prominent African American church. But, considering Dr. King's celebrity, a large crowd was expected. Ultimately the Scottish Rite auditorium located in downtown Fort Wayne with its seating capacity of 2,400, in close proximity to hotel accommodations seemed perfectly suited to host the event.

On May 1, 1963, Fort Wayne *Journal-Gazette* staff writer Wesley Bashore published an article informing their readers that Dr. Martin Luther King had accepted the invitation to speak. The invitation had been extended by an eclectic group of city dignitaries, including the Frontiers Club, a leading African American civic organization. Among their distinguished members was trailblazing educator Dr. Levan Scott. A Muncie native and 1958 graduate of Ball State University, Dr. Scott worked as an elementary school teacher, consulting teacher, and assistant principal at Central High School before being hired as principal at McCulloch Elementary School in 1963. His promotion elevated him to become the first black principal in Fort Wayne Community Schools.

Other active club members instrumental in Dr. King's invitation included local dentist and Frontiers Club member Dr. Allan Wilson. William Watson, dean of boys at the predominantly black Central High School, and welfare department associate Albert Coleman were also active members of the committee tasked with courting Dr. King to speak in Fort Wayne, as was First Presbyterian Pastor John Meister.

Reverend Meister had developed a progressive reputation in town. Meister was a white, pro-Civil Rights religious leader who, by the mid-1960s, had welcomed at least twenty black families into First Presbyterian, a thriving downtown place of worship. His sons, Peter and Greg, recalled that their socially active father was known for communicating to prospective white families that if they disapproved of an integrated congregation, they needed to find a new church.

In addition to Rev. Meister, members of the Fort Wayne clergy from multiple races and faiths publicly supported King's appearance. Bishop Leo Pursley of the Fort Wayne-South Bend diocese, Dr. Donald Bailey, district superintendent of the Methodist church, and Rev. John Dixie were among those who commended the Frontiers Club invitation. Although this diverse mixture of Fort Wayne spiritual leaders supported an appearance by the nation's preeminent Civil Rights leader, some local white citizens did not embrace the invitation, and publicly voiced their concerns.

4

Delays and Threats

The speech was originally scheduled for May 28, 1963. Bloodshed in Birmingham burdened Dr. Martin Luther King's schedule, necessitating a change. His Fort Wayne appearance was rescheduled for June 5, 1963. From the moment his expected arrival was publicly announced in the both city newspapers, the *Journal-Gazette* and the *News-Sentinel*, city residents split either in favor or opposition of his visit.

A letter to the editor appearing in the May 21, 1963 issue of the *News-Sentinel* echoed speculative claims from the FBI that King was a Communist and quoted several supporting statements from the *Advance Guard* newsletter from the Indiana Young Americans for Freedom, a national organization originated by conservative author and political commentator William F. Buckley. The writer, Fort Wayne resident Graham Grove, continues with his own input: "For the best interests of both the Negroes and whites of our nation, it is time that the true motives behind the actions of Rev. King be made known." In the May 23, 1963 issue of the *News-Sentinel*, Barbara Johnson of Fort Wayne raised similar questions, after listing several of King's associates with ties to Communism:

> I am sure there are millions of American people, both white and colored, who would like to know if Martin Luther King Jr. is interested in just the negro problem, or in the furtherance of Communism. Where does he get his income? Why is he opposed to the House Un-American committee?… I believe that a thorough investigation to the answers of these questions is far overdue.

Another writer asserted that "Fort Wayne, the conservative leader of the Midwest, has just sunk to an all-time low." Other citizens, however, enthusiastically supported Dr. King's visit to the Fort.

Dave Schwalm, a student from Carleton College in Minnesota, spoke for other progressive youths of his generation, and directly addressed in the May 23, 1963 *News-Sentinel*, a Mr. Tom Gross, who had also been critical of the King invitation. Schwalm wrote the following: "I am quite proud of Fort Wayne that they have invited Dr. Martin Luther King to speak.... You, Mr. Gross, don't have to go hear him. He won't gloss over the less aesthetic aspects of the United States as you would wish. He won't tell you what a wonderful country this is to live in. He won't wave the flag. Don't go, Mr. Gross, you wouldn't listen if you did..."

Another letter of support, written by city resident Bob Carlin, was published in the June 3, 1963 edition of the *News-Sentinel*. He directly addressed a previous letter to the editor written by Barbara Johnson. Summarizing, he writes: "First, Barbara Johnson, why are you so eager to discredit Mr. King? Are you interested first in fighting communism, or in keeping the Negro in his place? Do you deny that the Negro does have a just cause?" Later, he continues:

> Mr. King's forthcoming speech in Fort Wayne is being actively supported by clergymen of all faiths and by numerous other organizations which are just as concerned with the welfare of our nation as you could possibly be. These are not ignorant, uninformed people, but responsible citizens who believe in Mr. King, and his cause. You see, patriots are found on both sides of the fence, both conservative and liberal, and also down the middle.... Fort Wayne has already heard from Mississippi Governor Barnett. Now, in fair play, let's give Martin Luther King his chance to be heard.

These letters indicated that racial disagreements had escalated in Fort Wayne. Local Civil Rights activists such as Dr. Scott, local dentist and NAACP President Dr. Bernard Stuart, and Reverend Adams pushed local political and business leaders hard for an end to discriminatory practices, and an inception for equal opportunity for citizens of all races. Joe Adams, Rev. Adams eldest son, recalls his father targeting Fort Wayne movie theaters for full desegregation efforts. "In those days, blacks were required to sit in the balcony. We couldn't sit on the floor. Well, Dad got together with some of the kids and adults from church and worked to change that policy." During the late 1950s, Rev. Adams devised a children's campaign similar to what Dr. King utilized in Birmingham. He built a coalition of children to help desegregate the city. Rev. Adams and Rev. Jesse White also staged successful lunch counter sit-ins, and subsequent boycotts of several popular downtown restaurants that refused to serve blacks. Advocating for a level playing field for black citizens did not sit well with some Fort Wayne residents.

In April 1963, the Fort Wayne Police Department learned of a threat to "handle the negro problem of Fort Wayne." A letter surfaced, using newspaper clipping letters, threatening to burn down an African American house on Hanna Street near downtown. One month later, following the announcement of King's speech, a second letter was received and opened by young Scottish Rite secretary Kaye Ann Noack indicating involvement from the "Ku Klus Klan," which was misspelled by the sender. The writer of the letter promised to bomb the Scottish Rite during the night of Dr. King's speech and vowed "to drive the black man back to Africa." Police determined that both letters were written by the same individual. Additionally, Fort Wayne Police asserted that the Klan had not been active in the city for many years. Some residents of color differed in that assessment. The FBI became involved following the second letter.

Toward the end of May 1963, near the original May 28 date of Dr. King's speech, an additional letter from the "Ku Klus Klan" was received by Noack once again threating to bomb the Scottish Rite if King's speech continued as planned. "I knew about it, it could be a possible hoax," Noack recalled in a June 4, 2013 *Journal-Gazette* article written by staff writer, Ron Shawgo, "but you don't get worked up because you don't know if it's a hoax or not." Dr. Stuart would receive a similar threatening letter around this time.

A third and final letter was received by Noack on June 4, 1963, the day before the rally. Once again, the threat indicated a promise to blow up the Scottish Rite if the speech proceeded as planned. FBI agents added this similar letter to their file, but they were unable to identify any specific suspects to question. Considering the consistency and legitimacy of multiple threats, Mayor Burns, who was in Topeka, Kansas during the night of the SCLC rally at a previously scheduled conference, along with Police Chief Paul Clark, and Allen County Prosecutor Walter Helmke, agreed that a heightened police presence was warranted in order to ensure the safety of all citizens attending the rally, as well as for Dr. King and the rest of the SCLC leadership. For added security measures, detectives from the FWPD were ordered to accompany Dr. King before, during, and after the rally. Perhaps the additional precautions and police presence thwarted any violence. The summer evening of June 5, 1963 would prove to be peaceful.

The evening prior to the SCLC Freedom Rally, both Dr. King and Rev. Abernathy were interviewed by both the *Journal-Gazette* and the *News-Sentinel*. Published in the June 6, 1963 edition of the *News-Sentinel* written by Ernest Williams, King was asked to share his opinions on President John F. Kennedy's record on Civil Rights. "President Kennedy has done some significant things in the field of Civil Rights but hasn't done enough. He has not given the leadership the problem demands. There is a greater need now than ever before for moral persuasion on the part of the President."

Later, he suggested that Kennedy engage the American people in "fireside chats" similar to President Franklin D. Roosevelt during the Great Depression. He also urged that instead of taking trips abroad, Kennedy personally visit the south, and speak with their people, and their moderate leaders.

Reverend Abernathy weighed in when asked about the Birmingham campaign. "Our economic boycott during the Easter buying season was 98% effective. And the southern white man hurts most when he is hurt in the pocketbook." He continued: "What brought the whole moral question into focus were the hoses and police dogs loosed on little children. When these pictures appeared in this country, and throughout the world, pressure began to be put on the Birmingham whites by people of good will all over the nation."

When asked about full integration, and concerns among some Americans about an increase in inter-racial relationships, Dr. King replied: "The Negro wants to be the white man's brother, not his brother-in-law."

Finally, Dr. King was asked about the Malcolm X lead Muslim movement. It was common knowledge among most of the nation that Dr. King and Malcolm X disagreed over the optimum Civil Rights approach. King claimed that only 100,000 of America's 20 million black citizens identified with the Muslim movement. "And it won't have an appeal if we continue to work toward solution of the problem. But, if the problem is not solved, it can only serve to increase the strength and appeal of the Muslim movement."

When interviewed by Journal-Gazette reporter Wesley Bashore, King was asked to address recent conflict caused by Alabama Governor George Wallace. In a recent article written by Richard Rovers with *New Yorker* magazine, Rovers had asserted that a double standard of treatment existed with President Kennedy, suggesting that King received more legal leeway than Governor Wallace. "We are morally and constitutionally right in our civil disobedience to the unconstitutional law requiring a permit for parading," said King, referring to the recent arrest of himself and Rev. Abernathy, and their subsequent imprisonment in Birmingham.

In his article, Rovers had suggested that President Kennedy's recent actions with both leaders were inconsistent. While Dr. King was permitted, even encouraged, to defy a local parading ordinance in Birmingham, Governor Wallace was punished for failing to comply with a Federal order permitting black citizens to register at the University of Alabama. "Ours is a government of laws, not of men or force," Rovers wrote. Although King admitted that he was unaware of the article, he supplied a quick and logical rebuttal. "The local ordinance appears on the face of it to be constitutional, but it is being used to preserve racial segregation, which is against Federal law," King retorted. "Wallace proposes breaking the Federal law. We are engaged in civil disobedience to a local unconstitutional law while being engaged in civil obedience to a Federal law. Governor Wallace is engaged in civil disobedience to Federal law, as well as standing against that which is morally right."

Later, King was asked to compare and contrast racial differences between northern and southern states. Bashore suggested that most northerners tend to believe racial discrimination is limited to the southern states. "It just isn't true," King replied with dismay. "No section of this country can boast clean hands in the field of brotherhood. In the south, segregation has been legalized and overt. In the north, in cities such as this [Fort Wayne], it is illegal, but covert. The *de facto* segregation of the north, however, can be just as damaging as the previous legal segregation of the south." Instilling Fort Wayne residents with a sense of urgency to immediately rectify centuries of racial oppression would be the primary goal of Dr. King, and the SCLC during their visit.

5

Love Works Miracles

June 5, 1963. Dr. King's flight was late. Waiting impatiently in the airport concourse was a white, middle-aged man wearing a conservative business suit. A wooden baseball bat was gripped tightly in his hands. He tapped the bat incessantly on the concrete floor of Fort Wayne's Baer Field airport. He stood in solitude. Waiting anxiously, he stood near the city's welcoming committee, and carefully scanned incoming flights. Local journalists noticed him. So did FWPD chief Paul Clark.

The TWA flight from Chicago finally touches down at 5 p.m., June 5, 1963, a half-hour behind schedule. The hatch opens. Passengers move down the steps onto the tarmac. Reverend Adams and his committee walk purposefully toward Dr. King. So does the man with the bat. He inches closer to Dr. King. Moments before reaching the Civil Rights icon, Chief Clark intercedes and confronts the mysterious man. He sternly instructs him to leave the bat behind if he wishes to greet Dr. King. The man was dumbfounded. When questioned why he was carrying a baseball bat at the airport, in close proximity to Martin Luther King, the man laughs. He explains with surprise that he was recently given the bat by his employer for reaching his sales quota. "I wasn't even aware Martin Luther King was on that flight," he offers innocently.

The SCLC Freedom rally at the Scottish Rite auditorium was scheduled to begin at 8 p.m. Stepping out of the plane were SCLC Civil Rights leaders Wyatt Walker, Rev. Ralph Abernathy, and Dr. Martin Luther King. Greeting them were Reverend Adams, Dr. Allan Wilson, and John Nuckols, Fort Wayne's first black member of City Council, elected in 1959.

Following pleasantries, Reverend Adams whisked Dr. King away in his new Buick. Union Baptist Church was the first destination on the agenda.

Dr. King was given a tour of the recently constructed, red brick, midtown facility, and met with several church officials. Following the Union Baptist visit, Reverend Adams next planned to introduce Dr. King to an important Fort Wayne business leader.

Kelley automotive dealerships have successfully served Fort Wayne area residents motor vehicle needs for multiple generations, selling all GM brands, new and used. By 1963, Reverend Adams had purchased several automobiles from co-owner Jim Kelley at their Buick dealership on Calhoun Street, and had developed a friendly, reciprocal business relationship. Kelley was a generous donor, and occasional guest speaker at Union Baptist. Rev. Adams, impressed with the fair treatment he received from a prominent white businessman, frequently recommended Kelley Buick to members of his congregation. Following their tour of Union Baptist, Reverend Adams pulled into the Kelley Buick dealership to introduce his respected business acquaintance to his esteemed guest.

Retiring to his private office, Jim Kelley was joined by his brother and business partner Bob Kelley. The group chatted with Dr. King about his vision, and his goals for America. "He was a very impressive guy. He was very organized. He had a presence about him that was very unusual. He was more than a minister. He was a statesman," recalled Jim Kelley in a January 14, 2000 *News-Sentinel* article written by Kevin Kilbane.

Following their visit with the Kelley's, Reverend Adams arranged for King, Abernathy, and Walker to receive suites at the Hotel Van Orman located downtown, only two blocks from the Scottish Rite. The Van Orman was considered one of the more prestigious hotels in Fort Wayne. It also had a history of racial discrimination.

Harold Van Orman Jr., son of former Indiana Lieutenant Governor Harold Van Orman Sr., had owned and operated the Van Orman hotel, located at the corner of Harrison and Berry Street, behind Fort Wayne's famous Coney Island, since 1947. Van Orman also had ownership stakes in the Fort Wayne Komets hockey team, as well as the Fort Wayne Daises women's softball organization. His downtown hotel was a marvel. Its nine-story, 263-room structure was known for its ornate beauty, complete with a stunning stained-glass skylight, and beautiful interior marble walls. It was generally considered one of the more upscale and elegant establishments in the state of Indiana until its closing in 1969, and demolition in 1974. George Wallace, Eugene McCarthy, and future Presidents Harry S. Truman and John F. Kennedy were just a few of the famous people that once stayed at the Van Orman. Blacks were not allowed to rent a room at the establishment until challenged by Reverend Adams.

Van Orman and Rev. Adams had a fractured relationship. Joe Adams recalled one occasion when both men needed to be separated to prevent a physical confrontation after an argument escalated, and Van Orman called Rev. Adams a liar. Following multiple discussions between the two men, which included threats of boycotts and demonstrations with support from the Fort Wayne legal community, Rev. Adams successfully convinced Van Orman to begin renting rooms to blacks by the early 1960s. Van Orman would not, however, agree to serve blacks in their dining area. Undeterred, Rev. Adams solicited the help of a local judge who intervened and ordered the Van Orman to comply with Rev. Adams wishes.

Following their visit to the Kelley auto dealership, Rev. Adams drove Dr. King and Rev. Abernathy to the Hotel Van Orman. He located and addressed the owner directly. "Mr. Van Orman, I want two suites, and I want them complimentary." Van Orman offered no resistance, obliged Adams' request, and provided luxury suites, free of charge, to the prominent Civil Rights leaders. The SCLC leaders retired to their rooms to prepare for the evening rally.

As the time closed in on 8 p.m., multi-racial crowds of attendees by the thousands began filing into the Scottish Rite. Across the street from the main entrance stood a group of disgruntled white male protestors picketing the event. The group identified themselves as "Citizens for Equality through Separation." Members of the news media later identified the picketers as Jack Miller, Robert Miller, William Thatcher, and Richard Faith of Fort Wayne, plus Russell Oberley of Monroeville. A final demonstrator, Chuck Edgar of Fort Wayne, was later removed by Fort Wayne Police for failing to provide proper identification.

Jack Miller claimed to be the leader of the group. While interviewed by Van Lesley of the *News-Sentinel*, Miller made the following assertion: "… the Negro is not unequal in the eyes of God, but anthropologists have proven them to be intellectually, morally, and emotionally inferior." Following this statement, the reporter pointed out that renowned anthropologist Margaret Mead had scientifically proven recently that these differences between races do not exist. Miller responded that he had "never heard of her." Miller also suggested that the American government should provide 14 percent of its land mass for a separate "black state." The picketers continued their demonstration across the street from the Scottish Rite prior to the beginning of the rally, but never crossed in an attempt to enter the inside of the auditorium.

In addition to the picketers, a pickup truck flying a Confederate flag, and displaying out-of-state license plates, circled the outside of the auditorium multiple times. Police and city officials were on high alert following the rash of death threats, but neither group of dissenters engaged in violent activities.

An estimated audience of 3,000 multi-ethnic, multi-faith, multi-aged people filled the auditorium to standing room only. Approximately one-third of the crowd was white. Hundreds of people were turned away due to a lack of space in the auditorium. Speakers were provided to broadcast the event outdoors to those who were unable to sit inside. Those in attendance were given the opportunity to pay for membership to the SCLC, which allowed them to sit on the stage behind King, and other speakers. Future three-term Fort Wayne Republican Mayor Paul Helmke was one such individual who chose to pay the $1.25 required to join. Helmke, who had recently finished the ninth grade, was good friends with both Peter and Gregg Meister, sons of First Presbyterian Pastor, and co-organizer, Rev. John Meister. Helmke's desire to attend the Freedom rally stemmed from a healthy interest in current events, and discourse covering all sides of politics. "I was pro civil rights, but a Barry Goldwater supporter," Helmke recalled. "I enjoy hearing speakers all across the political spectrum." After paying their fees, Helmke and Peter Meister took seats near the end of the stage, facing the sellout audience, and the backs of all speakers.

Rabbi Frederic Doppelt, leader of the city's Jewish temple from 1939–1969, launched the program with the invocation. The Reverend Richard Mitchell of Associated Churches then provided the benediction. Combined choirs from Union Baptist, Plymouth Congregational, Pilgrim Baptist, and Turner Chapel churches then delighted the crowd with opening hymns.

Sporting a Roman Catholic priest collar, Reverend Meister took his turn at the podium. He surveyed the standing room only crowd through bright lights cascading over a darkened auditorium. The anticipation had reached a crescendo. Rev. Meister introduced the future Nobel Prize winner as a "glorious distributor of people and peace." The audience rose to their feet. The ovation was thunderous. The Reverend Dr. Martin Luther King Jr. gathered his thoughts and stepped confidently to his rightful place at the podium.

"There comes a time when a people get tired of injustice, oppression, exploitation. We want to be free," King declared with southern drawl in his typical measured and stoic demeanor to a raucous crowd. "The idea of freedom and human dignity's time has come. The Negro is no longer willing to accept segregation. It is sociologically untenable, politically unsound, and morally wrong. Segregation is the new form of slavery covered with the niceties of civilization." King proclaimed that the non-violent resistance movement in the south has given black persons "a new sense of dignity and self-respect after 300 years. He had come to feel that perhaps he was inferior. He has re-evaluated himself. The Negro today will suffer, sacrifice, even die to be free."

Addressing some common concerns and criticisms of the Civil Rights movement, King continued:

Some may say slow up, you're moving too fast. We can't—we love America too much. We're through with gradualism, tokenism, see-how-far-you've-come-ism. Now is the time to get rid of segregation. Now is the time to make the American dream a reality. We have learned to stand up against the evil system—and still not hate in the process. We have discovered that love works miracles.

"If you go to jail," he continued, referring to their recent experience in Birmingham, "you transform it from a jungle of shame to a haven of human dignity. We can say to our opponents we will match your capacity to inflict suffering by our capacity to endure suffering. We will wear your down with our capacity to endure suffering. We will win our freedom."

King later addressed the Civil Rights struggle on a global scale:

The race problem in the United States must be solved or the United States will be relegated to a second-rate power in the world. Our nation has a date with destiny. If moderation means pushing on toward the goal of meeting that destiny, then it is good. If it means slowing up, then moderation is a vice which all men of good will must oppose.

Addressing the use of non-violence to affect change as compared to a more aggressive approach from other Civil Rights leaders such as Malcolm X, King made the following assertions.

I'm still convinced that if the Negro succumbs to the temptation to use violence in the struggle for freedom, generations yet unborn will suffer the consequences. Non-violence should not be dismissed as a weak method. It works on the conscience. It enables us to stand before our most bitter opponents and meet their physical form with soul force.

Applause shook the foundation of the Scottish Rite. Never in the history of Fort Wayne has a speaker galvanized an audience with such an uplifting, spiritual experience. "Dr. King spoke with a quiet, commanding presence," Helmke fondly recalled. "There was a great feeling of love and reconciliation in the auditorium," Peter Meister remembered.

As men in suits began passing around collection baskets to the audience, Reverend Ralph Abernathy stepped to the lectern with strict instructions. "I don't want to hear any noise when this basket passes in front of you." Confused glances were exchanged with many guests, especially white attendees. "Folding money don't make no noise. Checks don't make no noise. Coins make noise. I don't want no noise!!" Laughter and knowing glances filled the auditorium as guests connected with Rev. Abernathy's instructions.

Following the end of the program, King, Abernathy, and Walker stayed behind briefly to shake hands, and sign autographs. One such autograph was signed for the future mayor. Dr. King signed the back of Helmke's SCLC membership receipt, an autograph that he still preserves in glass casing to this day, along with a copy of the 1964 *Time* magazine "Man of the Year" cover autographed for his father. Helmke considers these items to be among his most treasured possessions.

After departing the Scottish Rite, Rev. Meister had previously invited the SCLC leadership group back to First Presbyterian for a brief post-rally reception. King, perhaps fatigued following a long, eventful day, spent the majority of the reception quietly sitting off to the side sipping punch, commiserating with few people, Gregg Meister recalled.

Once the reception concluded, Rev. Adams transported the Civil Rights leaders to the Van Orman hotel for a late dinner. Central Standard Time now was approaching midnight. Rev. Adams recalled a late meal full of good spirited laughter and storytelling following a rally that exceeded expectations. The energetic, overflow crowd had donated in excess of $6,000 into the SCLC collection plate. This total easily eclipsed donations collected at recent rallies in much larger Midwestern cities such as Indianapolis and Cleveland. After dinner concluded, the group retired to their rooms for the evening. The Civil Rights leaders departed Baer Field airport the following morning. Rev. Martin Luther King would never return to Fort Wayne, Indiana.

6

The Nation, Second Half of 1963

A Dream Deferred?

Defiance, promise, hope, murder, uncertainty—only days after Dr. Martin Luther King's June 5 visit to Fort Wayne, the Civil Rights movement claimed significant victories, and setbacks. These events would shape the movement for the remainder of this turbulent year.

University of Alabama

She wanted to be an accountant; he dreamed of becoming a police officer. They both hoped to pursue their respective degrees at the University of Alabama. Vivian Malone and James Hood both attempted to enroll at the Tuscaloosa campus on June 11, 1963. Governor George Wallace refused their admission. The segregationist governor stood defiantly at the main entrance to the university admissions office, preventing the registration of the school's first African American students. Appeasing his voting base, Wallace criticized the "Unwelcomed, unwanted, unwarranted and force-induced intrusion upon the campus of the University of Alabama."

The Kennedy administration was prepared for Wallace's stand. Deputy Attorney General Nicholas Katzenbach, who accompanied Malone and Hood, placed a phone call to the White House. President Kennedy authorized Alabama National Guard intervention to enforce a Federal order to integrate the university. Four hours later, during the second attempt to register the black students, Wallace reluctantly stepped aside, allowing Malone and

Hood to complete the registration process. The following evening, June 12, 1963, President Kennedy addressed a nationwide radio and television audience, calling for an end to segregation and racial inequality:

> This nation was founded by men of many nations and backgrounds. It was founded on the principle that all men are created equal, and that the rights of every man are diminished when the rights of one man are threatened.... It ought to be possible for American consumers of any color to receive equal services in places of public accommodation ... it ought to be possible, in short, for every American to enjoy the privileges of being American without regard to his race, or his color. In short, every American ought to have the right to be treated as he would wish to be treated, as one would wish his children to be treated.... I am therefore asking the Congress to enact legislation giving all Americans the right to be served in facilities which are open to the public.... My fellow Americans, this is a problem which faces us all—in every city of the North, as well as the South.... This is one country. It has become one country because all of us, and all the people who came here had an equal chance to develop their talents.

Following JFK's address to the nation, Martin Luther King was pleasantly flabbergasted. He had grown frustrated with the Kennedy administration's minimal Civil Rights progress in order to maintain the Southern Democrat vote. Now Kennedy had decided to listen to his heart more than his advisers. After watching President Kennedy's address, Dr. King enthusiastically proclaimed with a baseball analogy: "Can you believe that white man not only stepped to the plate, he hit it over the fence!!"

Medgar Evers

Thousands of miles away from Washington, D.C., in Jackson, Mississippi, Civil Rights activist Medgar Evers was watching President Kennedy's promise for equal justice and opportunity with great interest and enthusiasm. So was local KKK member and businessman Byron De La Beckwith. The president's speech struck different chords with each man.

Growing up in heavily segregated Decatur, Mississippi, in the Deep South, Evers received his World War II draft notice to join the U.S. Army in 1943. He fought valiantly while stationed in Europe, which included courageous participation in the D-Day invasion at Normandy, France. He earned the rank of sergeant and was honorably discharged following victory for the American-led Allied forces in 1945. Evers returned home to Mississippi with expectations of preferred opportunities fitting a war hero. Evers was mistaken. He soon discovered that the dark hue of his skin afforded him no such opportunity, despite his military accomplishments. Discrimination continued to run rampant in Mississippi. On one occasion, Evers and five friends were physically forced away from voting booths, by a white mob, at gunpoint.

Despite his exposure to hateful bigotry, Evers excelled academically, professionally, and socially. After graduating from the all-black Alcorn State University with a degree in Business Administration, Evers later applied for admittance to the Mississippi University School of Law. He was denied.

After marrying college sweetheart Myrlie in 1951, and completing his business degree in 1952, Evers became a successful insurance agent for Magnolia Mutual Life Insurance Company. He also became active in the NAACP. Borrowing Martin Luther King's non-violent, civil disobedience approach, Evers once organized a black boycott of gas stations that refused to allow blacks use of their restrooms. "Don't buy gas where you can't use the restroom" bumper stickers were seen all over the area.

Throughout late May and early June 1963, Evers' activism caused multiple threats on his life. This included a Molotov cocktail thrown into the carport at his home on May 28, 1963, plus numerous threats following a local television appearance when he outlined his plans to increase opportunities for blacks in Jackson.

Byron De La Beckwith was also a veteran of World War II, where he received the Purple Heart. Returning home to Greenwood, Mississippi, De La Beckwith married in 1945, and had a son in 1946. De La Beckwith became a successful fertilizer and tobacco salesman. He also became a white supremacist. Following the 1954 Brown *v.* Board of Education decision, De La Beckwith joined the Citizen's Council, the local arm of the Ku Klux Klan.

De La Beckwith was angered by the President Kennedy's Civil Rights address. He detested the idea of integration and equal rights for black citizens. Medgar Evers was a charismatic and articulate Civil Rights leader, which made him dangerous in the eyes of De La Beckwith and other southern segregationists. During the early morning hours of June 12, 1963, just hours after the president's speech concluded, De La Beckwith drove to the Evers home in Jackson and hid in shrubs across the street. Evers pulled into his driveway. De La Beckwith identified Evers through his hunting scope, aimed his Enfield rifle, and fired a bullet that pierced the back of the Civil Rights leader. Evers' wife and children were still awake inside their home. After hearing the gunshot, Myrlie opened the front door and discovered her beloved husband crawling along their driveway, reaching the steps outside their front door. He collapsed in a pool of his own blood, in front of his wife and young children. Evers died within a half-hour of the shooting. He was thirty-seven years old.

Following two mistrials from all-white juries in 1964, De La Beckwith lived a free man for thirty years. He would not be convicted of Evers' murder until a new trial was ordered in 1994. De La Beckwith received a life sentence and died in prison in 2001.

Freedom Marches

By the summer of 1963, the concept of a large but peaceful march in the nation's capital honoring the 100-year anniversary of the Emancipation Proclamation had been discussed among Civil Rights leaders. Dr. King, NAACP leader Roy Wilkins, National Urban League President Whitney Young, CORE (Conference of Racial Equality) leader James Farmer, SNCC (Student non-violent coordinating committee) leader John Lewis, plus activist and primary planner A. Phillip Randolph organized the momentous event. The Black Muslim movement was not invited. On June 22, 1963, only three days after Medgar Evers was buried in Arlington National Cemetery, primary event organizers met with President Kennedy, Attorney General Robert Kennedy, and several aides to discuss details. The Kennedy administration held several reservations about a march for racial equality of this magnitude.

Organizers of the march disagreed over how the event should be structured. Some favored a civil disobedience approach similar to the effective lunch counter sit-ins and freedom rides, while others preferred a more conservative approach in order to maintain Congressional support. Randolph hoped to merge the group of strong personalities into a cohesive unit. The Kennedy administration feared violence would appear and escalate due to the anticipated size of the crowd, which could jeopardize pending Civil Rights legislation. He urged the leaders to cancel the march. "We want success in Congress, not just a big show at the Capitol," explained President Kennedy. Both King and Randolph insisted that the march would proceed, would bring positive attention to the Civil Rights movement, and assured the president that the event would be peaceful. Realizing the coalition was not going to back down, the president promised to privately support the demonstration.

Prior to the March on Washington meeting, the president, Bobby Kennedy, and Justice Department Attorney Burke Marshall met privately with Martin Luther King. FBI intelligence had been presented to the Kennedy's indicating Dr. King had relationships with Jewish Attorney Stanley Levinson and writer Jack O'Dell, both whom, through agency surveillance, were suspected by the FBI to be Communist sympathizers. Both of these men were two of King's most trusted advisers, and were heavily involved in SCLC planning, and fundraising. King agreed to take the matter under advisement but did not comply with the president's request to immediately cut ties with both men.

The following day, June 23, 1963, King and the SCLC leadership landed in motor city. They collaborated with a local group known as the Detroit Council for Human Rights, and organized a massive demonstration known as the "Walk for Freedom March," which followed a path down Woodward Avenue in downtown Detroit. Estimates totaled 125,000 people that, at the time, was one of the largest demonstrations in U.S. History.

Later, at Cobo Hall, Dr. King spoke before another standing room only crowd. King urged the city, and the nation, to take immediate action toward rectifying racial inequality and injustice. "Now is the time to transform this pending national elegy into a creative psalm of brotherhood. Now is the time to lift our nation from the quick sands of racial injustice to the solid rock of racial justice. Now is the time to get rid of segregation and racial discrimination..." He also would allude to a "dream" during this speech that would become more familiar two months later:

> And so I go back to the south not in despair. I go back to the south not with a feeling that we were caught in a dark dungeon that will never lead to a way out. I go back believing that a new day is coming. And so this afternoon, I have a dream. It is deeply rooted in the American dream.... I have a dream this afternoon that there will be a day that we will no longer face the atrocities that Emmitt Till had to face or Medgar Evers had to face, that all men can live with dignity...

King's thirty-five-minute speech was received joyfully in the overflow audience, which helped convince him to use similar phrasing during the March on Washington in August.

Known officially as the "March on Washington for Jobs and Freedom," an estimated 250,000 people descended on the mall in Washington, D.C., on a blistering hot afternoon, August 28, 1963. A. Phillip Randolph plus his trusted associate and veteran activist Bayard Rustin, and 200 volunteers, handled the majority of the event planning, which included ensuring adequate restroom facilities, drinking fountains, food tents, and first-aid stations for a quarter million people. Volunteers from Riverside church in D.C. made an estimated 80,000 cheese sandwiches to feed hungry marchers.

In this pre-internet era, invitations for marchers were distributed through printed flyers handed out at churches, civic organizations, labor unions, youth groups, and civil rights organizations around the country. Approximately $120,000 was raised through Urban League and NAACP chapters, along with hundreds of private donors to cover the majority of overhead costs needed for an event of this magnitude.

Attendees traveled to the nation's capital through multiple modes of transportation. Some drove, others took trains, some chose air travel, and many took more economically friendly bus trips. One of the more unique travelers was Chicago native Ledger Smith, known affectionately to many as "Roller Man," a professional roller skater. Wearing a sign displaying "Freedom" etched across the chest, Smith skated nearly 700 miles in ten days to D.C. The married father of three traveled in this manner not as a publicity stunt, but for symbolic purposes. "To dramatize the March, I did it in the slowest way possible," Smith recalled at the time. "Roller Man" encountered many well-wishers along the way offering him handshakes, and words of encouragement. Other observers were not so friendly. After arriving in the nation's capital, Smith recounted during an interview on WAMU radio station that one car tried to run him off the road while he skated through Fort Wayne. For most of the remainder of his trip, Smith was protected by convoys of cars driven by NAACP members.

Security for the March on Washington continued to concern the Kennedy administration, law enforcement, civic leaders, as well as march organizers. Rustin coordinated the use of 2,000 volunteer marshals to help ensure a peaceful gathering. President Kennedy ordered 4,000 National Guard troops on high alert. Area hospitals were also placed on high alert, as were several area judges in case mass arrests were necessitated. All area liquor stores were closed for the day. A Major League Baseball game between the Washington Senators and Minnesota Twins was cancelled. Despite minimal evidence, FBI director J. Edgar Hoover, who was not supportive of the Civil Rights Movement, labeled the March a Communist plot. He requested, but did not receive, authorization to wiretap telephones and hotel rooms of Dr. King and other Civil Rights leaders while lodging in the nation's capital.

Counter protestors such as the Ku Klux Klan and American Nazi party were another security concern. Intelligence received from law enforcement indicated both groups intended to disrupt the march, perhaps with violence. However, no serious confrontations were reported. Only three arrests were made during the entire event.

Hoover was not the only public official critical of the March on Washington. One of the most vocal critics was another Civil Rights leader—Malcolm X. The Black Muslim leader sarcastically referred to the demonstration as the "Farce on Washington." Malcolm X asserted that the Kennedy administration was in total control of the demonstration, and that Dr. King and other organizers were willingly complying like "puppets." Malcolm X traveled to Washington, D.C., intending to hold a press conference, and discourage marchers from participating, but it was held during the march itself, and received minimal press coverage.

Activists arrived from all corners of the country and assembled at the Washington monument. Large groups began marching with locked arms singing the Civil Rights anthem "We shall overcome" until arriving at the Lincoln Memorial. The rally began at 10 a.m. and lasted over three hours. Popular '60s folk singers Joan Baez, Bob Dylan, plus Peter, Paul, and Mary performed during the early hours of the rally. Hollywood celebrities including Marlon Brando, Charlton Heston, Burt Lancaster, Sidney Poitier, and Paul Newman either gave speeches, or offered their support through active participation in the event.

Dozens of Fort Wayne residents made the nine-hour bus ride to participate in the March on Washington, including Dr. Stuart. The size of the crowd and the magnitude of the event took him by surprise. "I was amazed. It was overwhelming," Stuart recalled during an August 21, 1993 *News-Sentinel* newspaper article. "It was elbow to elbow. It really felt like if you passed out, you wouldn't fall down because so many people were packed in around you." Stuart made arrangements to attend because "it was time for some deep changes in the fabric of our country. None of us could foresee how dramatic this was or what an impact it would have on our country."

While a festive atmosphere permeated the colossal audience, discord was occurring within the Civil Rights leadership. Several leaders objected during a spirited argument beneath the Lincoln Memorial stage to what was considered confrontational language in a speech prepared by SNCC leader John Lewis. At one point during the disagreement, Bishop Patrick O'Boyle threatened to walk off the stage if Lewis refused to tone down the language. As final speakers stalled for time, Lewis agreed to revise the language some found inflammatory.

Following an uplifting rendition of "How I got over" by popular gospel singer Mahalia Jackson, the highlight of the afternoon without question was a speech near the conclusion of the program delivered by Rev. Martin Luther King. Known commonly as the "I Have a Dream" speech, it is widely considered one of the most memorable, influential, and significant speeches in human history. After explaining to the American people, and the world, the purpose of the Civil Rights movement, recent successes, and the struggles that lay ahead, King offered cautious optimism for the future:

> I have a dream that one day this nation will rise up, live out the true meaning of its creed: "We hold these truths to be self-evident, that all men are created equal. I have a dream that one day on the red hills of Georgia, sons of former slaves and the sons of former slave owners will be able to sit down together at the table of brotherhood."

Later King addressed racism: "I have a dream that my four little children will one day live in a nation where they will not be judged by the color of their skin, but by the content of their character..." As the speech climaxes, King exudes the need for all of God's children, regardless of color or faith, to "allow freedom to ring … from every city and every hamlet, from every state, and every city…. Free at last, free at last, Great God almighty, we are free at last!!" It was King's finest moment, and the peak of the Civil Rights movement.

Barely over two weeks following the inspirational conclusion of the March on Washington, tragedy struck again in Birmingham, Alabama at the 16th Street Baptist Church, one of the most prominent black churches in the city. On Sunday, September 15, 1963, five black girls between the ages of eleven and fourteen were excitedly discussing the new school year, which had recently begun, as well as the upcoming church service. The girls looked forward to taking part in the adult service that morning as they made their way from the church basement to the church above. Just before 11 a.m., a bomb exploded beneath the church steps. Four of the young girls were killed instantly. Addie Mae Collins, Denise McNair, Carole Robertson, and Cynthia Wesley lie bloodied and dead underneath a pile of rubble. Addie's sister, Susan, survived the blast but was permanently blinded.

After learning of the bombing, Dr. King sent a telegram to Governor Wallace: "The blood of our little children is on your hands." Dr. King gave the eulogy at the funeral for the girls three days later.

The FBI launched an immediate investigation. They quickly identified four members of the local KKK as the likely suspects. This same KKK chapter was responsible for firebombing the Birmingham Trailways bus station during the 1961 Freedom Rides. However, inadequate physical evidence coupled with a reluctance of many people in the community to come forward made for a difficult case. The investigation ended in 1968 with zero indictments. The case was reopened in 1971 after it was discovered that the FBI had not properly shared information with local law enforcement. One suspect, Robert Chambliss, was convicted of murder in 1977. Two other suspects, Thomas Blanton and Bobby Frank Cherry, were not convicted until 2001 and 2002 respectively, and sentenced to life in prison. The final suspect, Herman Cash, died in 1994. He was never prosecuted.

On September 22, 1963, one week after the bombing at the 16th Street Baptist Church, multiple members of the Fort Wayne clergy, as well as area civic leaders, organized a sympathy march in memory of the deceased girls. An estimated 1,500 city residents participated in the silent march that began at the downtown YMCA and proceeded to the Allen County Courthouse for a thirty-minute multi-faith prayer session. Local NAACP leader Dr. Bernard Stuart led the march. Rev. John Meister, Rev. James White, Rabbi Seymour Weller, Rev. Richard Mitchell, Rev. James McGraw, Monsignor Stanley Manoski, Rev. George Wood, Rev. Clyde Adams, and Rabbi Frederic Doppelt were among the area religious leaders who participated in the march and prayer. Several of these men had recently attended and participated in the Martin Luther King led Freedom Rally at the Scottish Rite auditorium.

FBI Director J. Edgar Hoover and his G-men continued to vigorously pursue Civil Rights leaders, especially Dr. King, on the notion that the movement had been infiltrated by Communists. Hoover continued to push for wiretap authorization, especially when it became clear to FBI intelligence that Dr. King had not severed his relationship with suspected Communist sympathizer Stanley Levinson. On October 10, 1963, Attorney General Robert F. Kennedy relented, and approved the wiretaps.

During the remainder of his life, the FBI closely monitored Dr. King's movements. His home and business office telephones were routinely bugged, as were hotel rooms where he stayed while traveling. The surveillance was constant. At a November 1964 press conference, Hoover referred to King as the "most notorious liar in the country." When the FBI learned that Dr. King had been engaged in extramarital affairs, they used this information in an attempt to negatively impact his credibility. At one point, an anonymous letter was received at the SCLC that encouraged Dr. King to commit suicide in order to avoid public embarrassment once the affairs became public knowledge. Efforts to derail the Civil Rights movement consumed the FBI director, especially after Dr. King publicly denounced the Vietnam War in 1967. In the end, little if any evidence was uncovered that definitively proved Dr. King was a traitor involved in espionage activities.

JFK

By November 1963, and with the next presidential election looming one year away, the Kennedy re-election campaign began to focus on the critical state of Texas. Although Texas was the home state of Vice-President Lyndon B. Johnson, Texas was considered a swing state in the 1964 election. The re-election campaign agreed that an appearance by Kennedy might help edge the president toward crucial electoral votes.

On November 22, 1963, following an appearance at a Chamber of Commerce luncheon in Fort Worth, the president and First Lady Jackie Kennedy took a short flight to Dallas. After arriving at the airport, and greeting well-wishers, the president and first lady joined Texas Governor John Connally and his wife Nelly for a motorcade through downtown Dallas. The group was seated in an open, top-down, black convertible.

As the presidential motorcade turned off Main Street near Dealey plaza at 12:30 p.m., gunshots thundered from a nearby book depository. Two bullets struck the president in his head and neck. Governor Connally, who would later recover from his serious injuries, was struck in the back. Secret Service agents jumped aboard as the car rushed toward Parkland Memorial Hospital. At 1 p.m., President John F. Kennedy was pronounced dead.

Kennedy's body was soon transported to the airport. At 2:38 p.m., a grim Vice-President Lyndon B. Johnson was sworn in aboard Air Force One as the thirty-sixth president of the United States of America. A stunned, and bloodied Jackie Kennedy stood by his side during the ceremony.

Approximately one hour following the assassination, law enforcement arrested Dallas book depository employee Lee Harvey Oswald. Following intense interrogation efforts and background checks, Oswald was fingered as the likely suspect. On Sunday morning, November 24, 1963, Oswald was being transported from police headquarters to the county jail. This transport was being filmed on national television. As Oswald was being loaded into a waiting police vehicle, an assailant rushed forward, and fired a bullet point blank into Oswald's stomach. The shooter was later identified as local nightclub owner Jack Ruby. Oswald was pronounced dead two hours later at Parkland hospital.

Martin Luther King, like the rest of the nation, and the world, was stunned and saddened by the news of the president's death. "I am shocked and grief stricken at the tragic assassination of President Kennedy. He was a great and dedicated President. His death is a great loss to America, and the world. The finest tribute that the American people can pay to the late President Kennedy is to implement the progressive policies that he sought to initiate in foreign and domestic relations."

On Monday, November 25, 1963, President John F. Kennedy was buried at Arlington National Cemetery. A shattered nation struggled to regain its footing. As 1963 reached its conclusion, Civil Rights leaders resumed their struggle while collaborating with a new presidential administration.

Harlem Renaissance poet Langston Hughes once articulated both the hope of prosperity, as well as the agony of oppression in black America:

> *What happens to a dream deferred?*
> *Does it dry up like a raisin in the sun?*
> *Or fester like a sore, and then run?*
> *Does it stink like rotten meat?*
> *Or crust and sugar over like a syrupy sweet?*
> *Maybe it just sags like a heavy load*
> *Or does it explode?*

During his speech at the March on Washington, Dr. King instilled hope of better days for black Americans. As an explosive 1963 ended leading to an uncertain future, some wondered if Dr. King's dream had been deferred.

7

"We shall overcome" in Fort Wayne

A hurricane of social unrest swept through Fort Wayne, and the nation, during the 1960s. The Civil Rights movement was the eye of that storm. Following the lead of Dr. King, Fort Wayne dentist, and NAACP President Dr. Bernard Stuart attempted to steer the city through the ocean of social change.

Due to a long history of nationwide racial discrimination, Woolworth department stores were targeted only one week after Dr. King's appearance. Dr. Stuart and other city Civil Rights leaders led boycotts at the corporation's Southgate plaza location. Three months later, in September 1963, Dr. Stuart organized a demonstration outside the Indiana & Michigan Power company due to their failure to recruit and hire more than token minority candidates. After company officials agreed to meet with the NAACP leadership, the protests were called off.

Later that same month, on September 24, 1963, Dr. Stuart led a march of approximately 150 parents demanding elimination of segregationist policies, realignment of school boundaries, as well as demands for structural improvements, with the inclusion of black labor, to the predominantly black Central High School located in downtown Fort Wayne. Dr. Stuart also requested the formation of a nine-member, biracial committee to examine and rectify "problems of inequalities."

Continuing, Dr. Stuart pledged that the NAACP would invoke "any and all non-violent and peaceful means of demonstration" if the school board continued to drag their feet, claiming they had shown "extreme reluctance in dealing with the same situation in the past." Requests for these desired changes largely fell on deaf ears. The school board officially pleaded for "patience, your help, your cooperation, and your counsel."

Following these coordinated acts of civil disobedience, Dr. Stuart generated some local enemies. In October 1963, Dr. Stuart received several letters signed by "KKK" promising to bomb his home if he refused to cease and desist all city integration efforts. Letters were turned over to the FBI for investigation, but no arrests were made.

In May 1964, Dr. Stuart made news again as he joined over 1,000 demonstrators outside the Van Orman hotel, protesting an appearance from segregationist Alabama Governor and Presidential candidate George Wallace. Many picketers were Lutheran and Catholic seminarians from nearby colleges. Signs displaying "Students for human rights" were plentiful in what was described as the largest protest in the city's history, according to *Journal-Gazette* reporter Wesley Bashore. Fort Wayne Police prevented demonstrators from entering the hotel mezzanine, which caused a brief scuffle. Alternatively, demonstrators loudly sang "We shall overcome" outside the hotel door in an effort to drown out the governor's speech.

Prior to his arrival at the downtown hotel, Wallace delivered a speech at the Fort Wayne Country Club where he expressed his opposition to the pending Civil Rights bill launched one year earlier under late President John F. Kennedy. The bill, he claimed, "is only 10% civil rights, and 90% federal power grab. It is a bill that says 'discrimination,' but that word isn't defined in the bill. The meaning of 'discrimination' would be left up to some bureaucrat in Washington. It is going to affect every farm and home and labor union and school." Wallace also addressed accusations of bigotry under his administration. The governor insisted that segregation in Alabama "is in the best interest of both races." Wallace also insisted that he did not hold racist views. "I am not a racist. I've never despised anyone because of his color, his creed, or his origin. All mankind is made by a Supreme Being and anyone who despises a man because of his color despises the handiwork of God."

The governor of Alabama arrived at the Van Orman amid heavy security from local law enforcement personnel as they passed through the large gathering of protestors. Fort Wayne Police Chief Chester Rickets commended Dr. Stuart for leading a peaceful, non-violent protest involving him, the students, and NAACP members. When interviewed by *News-Sentinel* reporter Robert Thompson, Dr. Stuart insisted that they "laid down the law" at a recent NAACP meeting regarding non-violence. "… it [the protest] would have to be orderly, and that if anybody got into trouble, he would have to stand on his own," said Stuart. Shortly after Governor Wallace's arrival, an anonymous bomb threat was called into the Hotel Van Orman lobby. Wallace was immediately evacuated by law enforcement. Following a thorough search from the Fort Wayne Fire Department, no bomb was located.

Despite objections voiced by Wallace and a minority of political officials, the Civil Rights Act passed convincingly in the House of Representatives on February 10, 1964, and the Senate on June 19, 1964. With Dr. Martin Luther King at his side, President Lyndon B. Johnson signed the Civil Rights Act into law on July 2, 1964. This landmark legislation, termed by Dr. King as a "second emancipation," represented the apex of the Civil Rights movement. Federal law outlawed discrimination in the workplace based on race, color, religion, sex, or national origin. It also banned "unequal application of voter registration requirements." Literacy tests were not specifically addressed. The law outlawed segregation in all states, in all areas of public accommodation, such as theaters, parks, sports arenas, hotels, and restaurants. Private establishments were exempted. The law also enforced the desegregation of all public schools. More than fifty years later, this law continues to guide and impact our daily lives.

Although passage of the Civil Rights Act represented a monumental step forward in the Civil Rights movement, racist attitudes were not going to disappear with the stroke of the president's men. In Fort Wayne, shortly before the passing of the Civil Rights bill, two city apartment managers informed Mayor Harold Zeis they would never agree to rent to black tenants. In July 1964, a black family visited a home for sale in a white neighborhood. Following their visit, "welcome nigger" was spray painted on the front of the home. In November of that same year, a city restaurant manager was fined for refusing to serve black customers. Racial unrest in the Fort Wayne, similar to many American cities, continued throughout the decade. In 1966, it took a half-dozen marches of more than 600 people to convince Mayor Zeis to submit to pressure, and allow the first black citizen, Rev. Lawrence Wyatt, to serve on the Fort Wayne Community Schools Board of Education. During these marches, large bags of ice were dropped from the roofs of downtown buildings, retired Fort Wayne Community Schools teacher Mary Ray recalled in a 1999 *News-Sentinel* article written by Shannon King. One bag narrowly missed her twin children. Ray recalled telling her husband she would march no longer out of fear for her children's safety.

In the fall of 1969, parents of students enrolled in four city elementary schools boycotted for nine days until the leaders of the state's largest school system agreed to desegregate. Reverend Jesse White of Progressive Baptist Church led the movement. "My father was a courageous person," declared his son Marshall White, founder, and CEO of the Unity Performing Arts Foundation. Battling with Mayor Zeis—who was "Bull Connor stubborn" according to Marshall White—was an uphill battle, but eventually his father and other city Civil Rights leaders prevailed.

Total school desegregation was not achieved until 1971 with the closing of Central High School, and recent opening of several new school buildings spread throughout the city. This closing resulted in new boundaries with forced busing that angered both black and white families.

Unrest in Selma

Voter suppression targeting black citizens continued despite passage of the Civil Rights Act, especially in southern states. On February 18, 1965, in Marion, Alabama, local church Deacon Jimmie Lee Jackson joined a group of an estimated 500 people demonstrating peacefully against voting inequities. After being confronted by the police, streetlights mysteriously went black, causing a melee between police and protestors. In the chaos, Jackson's eighty-two-year old grandfather was beaten with a nightstick. While coming to the aid of his grandfather, Jackson was beaten and shot by an Alabama state trooper. He died nine days later. Jackson was twenty-six years old and unarmed. Deeply angered by this incident, leadership from the SCLC and SNCC soon descended on the nearby city of Selma. Following debate between the two groups, a 54-mile march was planned from Selma to the state's capitol of Montgomery in an attempt to directly confront Governor Wallace for the killing of Jackson, and the continuation of voter suppression. Wallace denied their permit to march.

Sunday, March 7, 1965, SNCC leader John Lewis and Hosea Williams from the SCLC, led an estimated group of 600 Civil Rights activists, two per row to begin their journey toward Montgomery. As they crossed the Edmund Pettis bridge, a heavily armed group of Selma police, and Alabama state troopers were waiting. Once the group was less than 50 feet from law enforcement, troop commander Major John Cloud raised a bullhorn and informed the group they were engaged in an illegal march and ordered them to disperse to their homes, or churches. None of the marchers moved. After one minute, police and troopers bull rushed peaceful demonstrators like a brigade of soldiers attacking an enemy camp, pushing them back across the bridge. Tear gas was released. Police officers on foot and horseback beat dozens of marchers with bullwhips and billy clubs on what would become commonly known as "Bloody Sunday." Lewis was beaten unconscious and nearly killed. The brutality was captured on live television and by newspaper photographers. Some television stations interrupted their scheduled programming to broadcast the horror live, shocking Americans across the nation. Over the next forty-eight hours, demonstrations in support of the marchers erupted in eighty American cities. The White House was inundated with phone calls and telegrams demanding intervention.

Although many Americans were outraged at the carnage that occurred on the Edmund Pettis bridge, witnesses and reporters noted that some nearby white Selma residents cheered and encouraged the police while they savagely abused protestors. On national television, Selma Mayor Joe Smitherman blamed "Martin Luther Coon" for the agitation in his city. In an effort to avoid additional bloodshed, President Johnson began negotiating with Governor Wallace, as well as Dr. King.

Two days later, on March 9, 1965, Dr. King led a second march to the bridge in what would come to be known as "Turnaround Tuesday." Activists expected and were prepared for confrontations similar to the previous Sunday. However, SCLC attorneys appealed to U.S. District Court judge Frank Johnson Jr. in an attempt to overturn Wallace's blockade of the peaceful march. Judge Johnson agreed to hear the petition, but in the meantime, issued an injunction preventing future marches. With more than 2,000 marchers present, Dr. King led activists to the Edmund Pettis bridge. However, before again confronting local law enforcement, Dr. King commanded the group to kneel in prayer, then turn around, and return to their churches.

On March 15, 1965, President Johnson addressed a joint session of Congress, which was carried live on national television. Johnson called on Congress to pass the Voting Rights bill designed to end all voter suppression, including but not limited to poll taxes and literacy tests. The president concluded his call to action by borrowing from the Civil Rights movement's popular rallying cry. "It is wrong, dead wrong, to deny any of your fellow Americans the right to vote in this country. Their cause must be our cause too," the president continued. "Because it's not just Negroes, but it's really all of us who must overcome the crippling legacy of bigotry and injustice. And we shall overcome." While watching the national address, several SCLC officials cheered loudly. Dr. King watched quietly with tears streaming down his cheeks. Two days later, following assurances from LBJ that the marchers would be protected by the National Guard, Judge Frank Johnson ruled that demonstrators had a right to conduct their 54-mile trek from Selma to Montgomery. In order to ensure their safety, President Johnson solicited the help of 2,000 national guardsmen.

The five-day march to the Alabama state capitol began March 21, 1965. An estimated 25,000 people took part in the historic journey from Selma to Montgomery. The National Guard lined both sides of the road during the journey, in addition to helicopter cover overhead. Bob Long, a former member of the clergy at First Presbyterian was one participant. Ironically, Long and his wife moved from Fort Wayne the very day of Dr. King's appearance. Long, who once had a "wonderful experience" leading service for a black congregation at Union Baptist, bumped into another prominent Fort Wayne Civil Rights advocate on the road to Montgomery—Dr. Allan Wilson. Yet another marcher was future Fort Wayne resident Richard Kelsaw.

Born and raised in the tiny rural town of Coy, Alabama located 40 miles south of Selma, Kelsaw, like many other area residents, were outraged at the violence witnessed on "Bloody Sunday." Seventeen years old at the time, Kelsaw became motivated to march toward Selma with Dr. King, and thousands of other activists. "We started marching about eight in the morning until about four in the evening. We camped out in big pastures at night," he recalled during a 2018 interview published in Fort Wayne's *Ink Spot* magazine. "Martin Luther King and the SCLC provided food for everybody ... there were huge tents. The military put them up because when we camped out, the National Guard was all the way around the tents. We were very well protected from start to finish."

Upon arrival at the state capitol in Montgomery, Dr. King delivered a speech overflowing with optimism for the thousands of weary, but joyful marchers. "The end we seek is a society at peace with itself, a society that can live with its conscience.... I know you are asking today, how long will it take? I come to say to you this afternoon however difficult the moment, however frustrating the hour, it will not be long."

Following the courthouse rally, Kelsaw and the other marchers began heading for home, and providing rides to those in need. Kelsaw hopped a ride with Rev. Leon Riley and several other people. While riding down the same highway where they had just marched, a young black man, later identified as nineteen-year-old Leroy Morton, was running down the highway frantically yelling. He informed Kelsaw and the other riders that a woman who was driving him back to Selma had just been shot and murdered in his presence. "We were on the truck, and he was running down [the road] ... it had just happened," Kelsaw recalled. "He was running down the middle of the highway. We picked him up in a big truck ... cotton truck ... lots us on that truck. So we picked him up on that highway and went to Selma. When we got there, I don't know how but the FBI was waiting on us, and they talked to him." The victim was later identified as Viola Liuzzo, a female white Civil Rights activist from Michigan. Three members of the local KKK were later arrested and convicted in connection with the murder.

The Voting Rights Act passed both houses of Congress and was signed into law by President Johnson on August 6, 1965. The act outlawed all discriminatory voting practices, including poll taxes and literacy tests, for all American minorities.

In November 1965, Kelsaw and his family migrated to Fort Wayne to escape the intense racism, and brutal heat of the Deep South in addition to a desire to explore better job opportunities. Joining other family members who had already settled here, Kelsaw worked at a General Motors plant in nearby Defiance, Ohio, for nearly forty years until retirement. He still resides in Fort Wayne to this day where he is a loyal member of the local MLK club.

In March 1968, Dr. King flew to Memphis, Tennessee, to intervene in a quarrelsome sanitation workers strike. Demonstrations became heated, sometimes leading to violence. During the evening of April 3, despite battling illness, Dr. King articulated an unforgettable speech to an overflow crowd at Bishop Charles Mason Temple in downtown Memphis. "Well, I don't know what will happen now. We've got some difficult days ahead. But it really doesn't matter with me now because I've been to the mountaintop. And I don't mind." Dr. King paused briefly after loud applause and began to inadvertently foreshadow his immediate future. "Like anybody, I would like to live a long life. Longevity has its place. But I'm not concerned about that now. I just want to do God's will. And he's allowed me to go up to the mountain. And I've looked over. And I've seeeeeen the promised land." More applause, another short pause. "I may not get there with you. But I want you to know tonight, that we as a people, will get to the promised land! And so I'm happy tonight. I'm not worried about anything! I'm not fearing any man! Mine eyes have seen the glory, of the coming of the Lord!"

Dr. King would never give another speech. At 6:01 p.m. the following evening, April 4, 1968, one of God's most treasured gifts to humanity was extinguished from the Earth. King was standing on a balcony at the Lorraine motel in Memphis chatting with associates. Suddenly, an assassin's bullet ripped a hole in his chest, forever piercing a hole in the Civil Rights movement and the American dream. Martin Luther King was dead. He was thirty-nine years old.

Most heavily populated cities in America experienced rioting following the assassination of Martin Luther King. Several cities, including Detroit, Washington, D.C., Baltimore, and Chicago, resembled war zones. More than 20,000 people were arrested nationwide. More than 3,000 injuries were reported. Forty-three people died. Indianapolis was one of the few densely populated American cities that remained free of violence. Presidential candidate Robert F. Kennedy, who had been campaigning that day in Indiana, presented the tragic news to a predominantly black audience in a downtown urban park in the state's capitol. His extemporaneous speech is credited with maintaining peace in the city. "Martin Luther King to love and to justice for his fellow human beings, and he died because of that effort." Kennedy later acknowledged their feelings of rage while comparing the MLK and JFK assassinations. "For those of you who are black, and are tempted to be filled with hatred and distrust at the injustice of such an act, against all white people, I can only say that I feel in my own heart the same kind of feeling. I had a member of my family killed, and he was killed by a white man." As Kennedy empathically concluded his speech, he pleaded with the audience for peace: "What we need in the United States is not division. What we need in the United States is not hatred. What we need in the United States is not violence or lawlessness, but love and wisdom and compassion toward one another, and a feeling of justice toward those who still suffer within our country whether they be white, or they be black.... Let us dedicate ourselves to that, and say a prayer for our country, and for our people." Standing in the park where Kennedy delivered this eloquent speech is a statue of King and Kennedy reaching toward each other in a gesture symbolic of the ongoing quest for racial unity.

Fort Wayne was spared violent unrest. On Sunday April 7, 1968, during what President Johnson declared a national day of mourning, Fort Wayne held a memorial service for the fallen Civil Rights leader similar to other services held around the nation. An estimated 3,000 Fort Wayne residents marched one mile downtown in a silent procession from Pilgrim Baptist Church until arriving at the Allen County Courthouse on Main Street. Rev. John Dixie served as master of ceremonies. During the service, local NAACP leader Rev. Theodore Hudson proclaimed that Dr. King was "the best friend America ever had—especially white America." Rabbi Frederic Doppelt declared Dr. King a "modern day Moses leading his people to the promised land. The life of Martin Luther King was a holy moment in the conscience of humanity." Rev. Frank White from 1st Presbyterian, who once had a brick thrown through his window due to his support for Civil Rights, said of Dr. King: "When dreamers speak, they call our eyes away from our feet." The large crowd also joined Rev. Jesse White singing "Take my hand, precious Lord," Dr. King's favorite hymn.

John Nuckols

The '60s turned into the '70s, and struggle for Civil Rights continued, both nationally and locally. Following the tragic death of Martin Luther King, a new national leader never fully emerged to replace the irreplaceable. Progress throughout the '70s was illustrated through a series of events and individuals. African American males were elected mayors in major cities such as Cleveland and Atlanta. Increased representation occurred in state legislatures around the country, and in the U.S. Congress.

Fort Wayne once again represented a microcosm of the country. Progress was evident, but so were race-related conflicts. John Nuckols was often leading the charge toward closing the gap on racial inequality and discrimination throughout the decade.

Elected as the first black member of the Fort Wayne city council in 1959, Nuckols would serve twenty-two consecutive years until his death in 1982. Frustrated with Fort Wayne's modest progress in the arena of minority hiring under Mayor Robert Armstrong's administration in the late 1970s,

Members of the Frontiers Club pose with national Civil Rights leaders. *From left to right*: Dr. Levan Scott, Dr. Martin Luther King, Rev. Ralph Abernathy, and Dr. Allan Wilson. (*Journal Gazette, Fort Wayne, IN*)

Some local residents picketed Dr. King's 1963 visit to the Summit City. *From left to right*: Richard Faith, Robert Miller, William Thatcher, Russell Oberley, and Jack Miller. (*Journal Gazette, Fort Wayne, IN*)

Rev. Jesse White. (*Photo courtesy of Marshall White*)

Thousands of city residents, young and old, black and white, attended a memorial service in downtown Fort Wayne three days after the assassination of Dr. King, on April 7, 1968. (*Journal Gazette, Fort Wayne, IN*)

Aerial view of the large crowd of city residents assembling on Main Street in downtown Fort Wayne for a memorial service following the death of Martin Luther King. (*Journal Gazette, Fort Wayne, IN*)

Rev. Joh Meister. (*Photo courtesy of Peter Meister*)

Dr. Martin Luther King speaks to a capacity audience at Fort Wayne's Scottish Rite auditorium, June 5, 1963. (*Journal Gazette, Fort Wayne, IN*)

Alabama Governor George Wallace speaks at the Van Orman hotel in downtown Fort Wayne, May 2, 1964. (*Journal Gazette, Fort Wayne, IN*)

Hundreds of city residents picketed outside the Hotel Van Orman during Governor Wallace's speech on May 2, 1964. (*Journal Gazette, Fort Wayne, IN*)

Fort Wayne Urban League President Robert Wilkerson (right) chats with National Urban League President Whitney Young (left) in this 1963 photo. (Journal Gazette, Fort Wayne, IN)

The Martin Luther King Club has served the Fort Wayne Community since 1985 honoring the legacy of Dr. King. (*Photo courtesy of mlkclubfw.com*)

Dr. King arrives at Fort Wayne's Baer Field airport (now known as Fort Wayne International airport) during the afternoon of June 5, 1963. *From left to right*: Fort Wayne City Councilman John Nuckols, Dr. Allan Wilson, Rev. Clyde Adams, Dr. Martin Luther King, and Rev. Ralph Abernathy. (*Journal Gazette, Fort Wayne, IN*)

Rev. Theodore Hudson (standing at podium) addresses the crowd during a memorial service in downtown Fort Wayne honoring Dr. King, April 7, 1968. (*Journal Gazette, Fort Wayne, IN*)

Former Fort Wayne Mayor Paul Helmke. (*News Sentinel, Fort Wayne, IN*)

On June 5, 2019, during the fifty-sixth anniversary of his father's visit, Martin Luther King III appeared in Fort Wayne to speak at the Embassy Theater. Here he poses at the entrance of the Dr. Martin Luther King Memorial bridge prior to brief remarks. (*Photo courtesy of WPTA TV, Fort Wayne, IN*)

The Lorraine Motel in Memphis, Tennessee. The balcony outside room #306 was the site of Dr. King's assassination on April 4, 1968. The motel now serves as our National Civil Rights museum. (*Photo from pixabay.com*)

Following a week of civil unrest during the summer of 2020, several city leaders participated in, with hundreds of city residents, a Unity walk starting at the Allen County Courthouse and concluding at the MLK bridge. Pictured on left in short sleeve white shirt is Mayor Tom Henry. City Police Chief Steve Reed (with bullhorn) addresses the crowd. Allen County Sheriff David Gladieux (in brown uniform) stands on the right. (*WPTA TV, Fort Wayne, IN*)

The Dr. Martin Luther King Memorial bridge lights up the evening sky near downtown in the Summit City. (*Photo courtesy of Brian Sirois*)

Fort Wayne resident Eugene Parker, one of the most prominent agents in professional sports, is pictured here. Parker died in 2016. (*Journal Gazette, Fort Wayne, IN*)

Nuckols solicited several Federal agencies to intervene and implement a proactive affirmative action plan designed to close the hiring gap. The Office of Revenue Sharing, a division of the U.S. Treasury Department, was tasked with overseeing the changes. The division ordered the city to implement affirmative action hiring practices or risk losing federal funding. It was recommended that corrective plans be submitted within ninety days.

"This is something we inherited, and we are attempting to resolve it," deflected Mayor Robert Armstrong in an April 10, 1979 *News-Sentinel* article. Although records showed that both the police and fire departments had hired in the vicinity of 15 percent minorities over the previous few years, it was noted in the report that a miniscule amount of blacks and women of all races held administrative positions. The Office of Revenue Sharing report also cited evidence that "suggest that minimal efforts have been made to recruit and hire females and that greater efforts must be made to hire minorities."

In an August 9, 1979 *News-Sentinel* article, shortly after the City of Fort Wayne submitted their report to the U.S. Office of Revenue sharing, Nuckols applauded the efforts of the city to right the equal opportunity ship. "The most recent plan, if it could or would be implemented fully, would mark a major step forward in this city from where we were last April," he said. However, Nuckols raised concerns about the execution of the plan. The plan proposed the establishment of an Affirmative Action and Equal Employment office within the city government. A chief officer would be appointed to oversee the office, and that individual would report directly to the Mayor. Nuckols, citing concerns about the chain of command, suggested that the chief officer have two assistants. Nuckols also raised concerns about the feasibility of the program, as well as overly ambitious goals articulated in the report.

Following the defeat of incumbent Robert Armstrong in the November 1979 Fort Wayne Mayoral election, responsibilities for implementing new Affirmative Action policies fell to the administration of newly elected Mayor Win Moses. Shortly after taking office, local minority and feminist groups were critical of the new mayor and threatened to involve multiple Federal agencies for failing to rectify the ongoing problem. Moses Administrative aide Mark Angel declared in early 1980 that the Moses administration was "committed" to hiring more minorities and women. Nuckols and area civil rights activists remained skeptical. Rev. James Hall accused the new mayor of "tokenism" regarding minority hiring. Nuckols promised at a January 1980 press conference that "We'll fight until hell freezes over to get Affirmative Action in the city of Fort Wayne."

By August 1980, Nuckols had become increasingly frustrated with the Moses administrations minority hiring ineptitude. During a mid-August council meeting, Nuckols and Moses became entangled in a spirited disagreement over proper compliance. Nuckols admonished the mayor repeatedly for "not following that book," referring to a U.S. Treasury Department booklet in front of him outlining the city's new Affirmative Action directive. Nuckols pointed out that guidelines called for the creation of a separate department with a director in charge of monitoring city compliance with Affirmative Action policy. The debate became increasingly intense leading Moses to angrily slap the table, insisting that his office was meeting their obligations. Nuckols responded: "Don't you slap that table at me!" Both continued heated disagreements over the new policy. When Moses insisted that the new office could not be created until 1981, Nuckols stood up, declared "That's not good enough for me, Mayor," and abruptly left the meeting. Nuckols helped organize a local rally a few days later designed to apply additional pressure on Mayor Moses to create the new Affirmative Action office.

Thanks largely to the leadership of Nuckols, Affirmative Action eventually was fully implemented into the city government. Minority citizens are now afforded opportunities for city jobs that did not exist in prior generations.

Ku Klux Klan in Fort Wayne

The Ku Klux Klan, the domestic terrorist group known primarily for their hatred of blacks, Jews, Catholics, and homosexuals, once played a prominent role in Indiana politics. During the early and mid-1920s, KKK Grand Dragon D. C. Stephenson, who once boasted "I am the law in Indiana," commanded substantial influence in state politics. Indiana claimed one of the nation's largest KKK memberships. Stephenson was friends with Indiana Governor Ed Jackson and several members of the state legislature. Stephenson lobbied for Klan sponsored legislation, including a bill that would have prohibited Catholic nuns from wearing traditional "religious garb" while teaching in schools. The bill failed to pass.

Klan membership began to decline by the end of the 1920s following a sexual assault and second-degree murder conviction against Stephenson. His trial also unearthed a number of political scandals. Additionally, multiple newspapers, labor unions, and religious leaders denounced the organization.

Following the successes of the Civil Rights movement during the 1960s, membership in the KKK dwindled substantially nationwide, as did their political influence. During the late 1970s, KKK leadership was in the process of reinventing themselves with a gentler image, and attempted a comeback both nationally and in Fort Wayne. A June 26, 1978 article appearing in the *News-Sentinel* reported on a Klan luncheon held at a city hotel conference room. It was the group's first meeting since being re-chartered. Seventeen individuals who identified themselves as members of the KKK attended along with their wives and children. Several members insisted to *News-Sentinel* reporter that the Klan had progressed with the times.

"People think we're a bunch of drunken hillbillies, but we're not. The Klan's different now," said a Klan member in attendance who wished not to have his name revealed. The keynote speaker at the event was Indiana's Grand Dragon Jesse Jent from Anderson. Jent insisted that the Klan was not the violent organization of the past but were far from passive. "We don't look for violence, but we'll take whatever steps we have to." He characterized Klan members as "free, white, conservative Americans."

The local organizer of the event, a Vietnam War veteran who also did not wish to be identified, claimed that the KKK was not an overtly racist organization. "We're not against the blacks, we just don't think the government should force whites to socialize with them." Unrobed Klan organizers held the luncheon in the private hotel conference with open doors until a busboy mocked Klan members walking by the entrance wearing a white linen tablecloth thrown over his body. One frustrated Klansman rose and abruptly closed the door.

In early 1979, it was learned that Robert Hagadorn, who had been appointed to the position of committeeman for a Republican precinct on the northwest side of the city, was the leader of the local KKK chapter. City council member Win Moses, and challenger for the upcoming mayoral race, stated in a February 26, 1979 *News-Sentinel* article that it was "absolutely unforgiveable" that the Armstrong administration had not required Hagadorn to resign his post. One month later, he did resign under pressure. He also resigned from the KKK. The following year, Hagadorn, citing his KKK involvement as "a thing of the past," sought the office of GOP committeeman. He was defeated.

Vernon Jordan

Martin Luther King was not the only prominent Civil Rights leader to travel to Fort Wayne for a speaking engagement. In 1980, National Urban League President Vernon Jordan was invited to speak at the Fort Wayne Urban League annual dinner. He was arguably the most influential American black leader to visit the city since Dr. King's 1963 trip.

Jordan was born in Atlanta, Georgia, in 1935. He and his brother Windsor were raised by their parents, Mary and Vernon Sr., in the segregated south. After being denied an internship with an insurance company due to his race, the high school honors student earned money through various odd jobs, including chauffeur to former Atlanta mayor Robert Maddox. He attended college in the state of Indiana at DePauw University, graduating in 1957 with a degree in political science. Jordan was the lone black graduate. He then earned his law degree at Howard University in 1960. Upon graduation, Jordan, an imposing figure at 6 feet 4 inches with athletic build, immediately joined the Civil Rights movement. Throughout the '60s, and into the early '70s, Jordan served as field secretary for the Georgia NAACP, director of the Southern Regional Council for the Voter Education Project, and director of the United Negro College Fund. Jordan was elected president of the National Urban League in 1972.

On May 28, 1980, Jordan was invited to give the keynote address at the Fort Wayne Urban League's annual dinner at the Marriott hotel on the city's north side. Speaking before an estimated crowd of 450 people, Jordan discussed America's challenges militarily, economically, and domestically. Jordan also provided cause for optimism. "I believe that it's darkest before the sunshine, and so I believe in my country and its system, both politically and economically, and if it can be made to work for some of us, it can be made to work for all of us."

Following the conclusion of his speech, Jordan accompanied local Urban League board member Martha Coleman for a late dinner. Upon his return to the hotel front entrance around 2 a.m., the forty-four-year old National Urban League President stepped from Ms. Coleman's vehicle. Three bullets were fired toward Jordan from several hundred feet away by an unknown assailant. One bullet penetrated his back between his pelvis and chest. Jordan slumped to the ground. After consoling Jordan, Coleman rushed into the lobby and urged a clerk to call 911. Jordan was transported via EMS to Parkview Memorial Hospital minutes later with his life hanging in the balance.

Parkview called a black surgeon into emergency action. Dr. Jeffrey Towles captained the team that operated on Jordan. The primary bullet missed Jordan's spine by only a few centimeters and blew a hole through Jordan's back and chest the size of a human fist. Following multiple surgeries lasting several hours, Dr. Towles and his team were able to save Jordan. Dr. Towles later remarked this was the worst gunshot injury he had ever seen and commented how fortunate Jordan was to survive the assassination attempt.

Following the attempt on Jordan's life, leading Fort Wayne officials were deeply concerned about the threat of a race riot in the city. After a tense first few days following the shooting, the city remained quiet with no major disturbances.

After improving to a more stable condition, Jordan was visited by President Jimmy Carter. This visit would become the inaugural story aired on Ted Turner's new twenty-four-hour cable news channel, CNN. Senator and Presidential candidate Ted Kennedy, Civil Rights leader Reverend Jesse Jackson, and Gary Mayor Richard Hatcher also visited Jordan following the shooting. Rehabilitation and physical therapy lasted several months until Jordan fully regained his strength. During a *Washington Post* interview five months later, Jordan recalled his emotions at the time. "I obviously thought right after I was shot that I was going to die, and I didn't." he recalled. "I was conscious from the time I was shot until they put me under. Most of that is indescribable, personally. There was the fear of death, but also the reality of death abates a fear, especially under a situation I couldn't do anything about."

Following an exhaustive investigation, white supremacist Joseph Paul Franklin was formally indicted on June 3, 1982, more than two years after the shooting. Franklin was a drifter with ties to the American Nazi party and the KKK. In August 1982, Franklin was acquitted on all charges due to limited evidence tying him to the murder attempt.

Franklin had been on the FBI's radar for more than a decade. Following a trail of hate crimes that usually targeted black citizens, and occurred in multiple states, Franklin was finally tried, convicted, and sentenced to life imprisonment. While imprisoned, Franklin admitted during an interview with a *St. Louis Post-Dispatch* reporter in the late 1990s that he was indeed the individual who attempted to take Vernon Jordan's life in Fort Wayne in May 1980.

Franklin had been stalking Reverend Jackson in the Midwest with the intention of assassinating the Civil Rights leader. After his plan failed to gel, Franklin admitted that he next planned the Jordan murder after learning of his scheduled Urban League speech in Fort Wayne. Waiting patiently under a cover of darkness, the serial killer hid in tall grass along a highway, several hundred feet from the Marriott hotel entrance, armed with a hunting rifle and attached scope. When the National Urban League president returned to the hotel around 2 a.m., Franklin fired three shots. Police later determined that two of the bullets ricocheted off a nearby chain link fence, leading to minor shrapnel damage in Jordan's leg. The near fatal blow cleared the fence cleanly and struck Jordan in the back.

Franklin was executed in Missouri November 20, 2013 after admitting to multiple murders and murder attempts, including an attempt on the life of *Hustler* magazine editor Larry Flynt, an attempt that left him paralyzed from the waist down and wheelchair bound for life. Every shooting was racially motivated.

After making a full recovery, Vernon Jordan continued to rise in the ranks of the nation's political hierarchy. Perhaps the highlight of his career was working on the White House staff of President Bill Clinton, a friend of his, during the 1990s. Jordan returned to Fort Wayne on just one occasion.

Forever grateful for saving his life, Jordan and Dr. Jeffrey Towles remained lifelong friends. A Fort Wayne resident for sixteen years at the time of the 1980 shooting, Dr. Towles expressed dismay at the time of the Jordan shooting that a racially motivated hate crime could occur in his hometown. "I was appalled that the violence could happen in this town. It isn't the kind of place where they burn a cross on your lawn."

The two men maintained contact until Dr. Towles died in 2004. Jordan returned to Fort Wayne to attend the funeral for the doctor and friend who saved his life.

Rev. Jesse White

Known for his thick build, bushy sideburns, and commanding baritone voice, few leaders have ever commanded the power and influence in Fort Wayne as the Reverend Jesse White. Inspired by early Civil Rights activists such as Dr. King, and later developing a close friendship with Reverend Jesse Jackson, Reverend White attacked racial injustices head-on in the Fort for several decades.

Born and raised in Mississippi, White relocated to Fort Wayne during the mid-1950s to begin a ministry at Progressive Baptist Church. The charismatic minister would not, however, become deeply involved in local Civil Rights advocacy until the late 1960s, following the death of Dr. King. His first successful venture was the boycott of Fort Wayne Community Schools to protest a failure to integrate.

Following a bitter power struggle, Reverend White founded True Love Baptist Church in 1974. While engaged in ministry at his new church, Rev. White continued to advocate against racial discrimination in the city. He organized demonstrations against area banks, department stores, and hospitals over segregation, discriminatory hiring practices, and economic inequality. As was par for the course during the Civil Rights movement across the nation, demonstrations against social injustices outraged some citizens. White's son Marshall recalls multiple occasions when crosses were burned on their front lawn. Never deterred despite threats on his life, Rev. White continued to push forward to enact change. "People have always shown a great deal of interest in my leadership," White affirmed in a 1982 *News-Sentinel* interview. "When people aren't shown justice, then their leader must stand up and lead."

During the early 1980s, national Civil Rights spokesman and future Presidential candidate Rev. Jesse Jackson was drawing nationwide attention. Jackson was once part of Martin Luther King's inner circle. He was present at the Lorraine Motel and had spoken with Dr. King moments before he was assassinated in 1968. By the early '80s, Jackson had become America's leading Civil Rights advocate, heading the Chicago-based organization Operation PUSH (People United to Save Humanity). By the fall of 1982, Jackson coordinated a boycott of Anheuser-Busch for accusations of bigoted hiring practices. By the end of the year, K-Mart was on his radar for the same offenses. Jackson brought a boycott K-Mart campaign to Fort Wayne, working collaboratively with Rev. White.

Jackson, White, and several other local black clergymen developed Operation Breadbasket, a local initiative, under the SCLC umbrella, designed to target unlawful hiring practices in Fort Wayne. Rev. White was the organization's president. If the local boycott was unsuccessful, Jackson planned to organize nationwide boycotts, affecting over 2,000 K-Mart stores with 230,000 employees. Decisions were made to boycott a K-Mart store located in the predominantly black Southeast side of Fort Wayne. Demonstrations began in early December 1982 as the busy Christmas shopping season was in full swing. Thirty-five black citizens picketed outside both K-Mart entrances on a busy Saturday morning and afternoon. K-Mart store manager Paul Marhover was angry. "I don't know what that man's [Jackson] problem is," he declared to *News-Sentinel* reporters Kevin Leininger and Jerry Graff in the newspaper's December 6, 1982 issue. Corporate K-Mart officials expressed concern that demonstrations, like Anheuser-Busch, would lead to poor public relations on a national scale. "We're going to treat this as a local problem and try to have our local people solve it," pledged Robert Stevenson, K-Mart vice-president of public relations. Stevenson claimed telephone messages left with Operation Breadbasket officials had not been returned.

Rev. Jackson was invited by his close friend, Rev. White, to lead Sunday December 5, 1982 services at True Love Baptist Church. He preached the gospel to an estimated packed audience of 700, but also preached standing up for injustice. "Be smart, not K-Mart," Jackson urged the congregation. "You go to K-Mart, and ring that cash register and you feed the head of the snake that bites your head off." Following his sermon, Rev. Jackson further explained his concerns about corporate America to *News-Sentinel* reporter Kevin Leininger.

"Five out of six jobs are controlled by the private sector," said Jackson. "They get huge tax breaks, huge profits, invest in cheap foreign slave labor, but feel no obligation to revive the economy. Politicians are accountable to the public. Corporations aren't. We want trade, not aid. Parity, not charity." Jackson called for an investigation into K-Mart's minority hiring practices. "These companies have boycotted us. It's a policy of racism."

Hiring practices were carefully analyzed after the K-Mart boycotts concluded. Affirmative action policies were implemented. Following the success of the demonstrations, the relationship between Rev. Jackson and Rev. White blossomed. "My Dad and Jesse Jackson were good friends," recalled Marshall White. "We had him [Jackson] over to our house for dinner whenever he was in town." Rev. White also became President of Jackson's local PUSH chapter, and assisted him with his 1984 and 1988 Presidential campaigns. Both men continued to forge ahead on the highway toward racial equality. Despite facing numerous detours and roadblocks along the way, they encouraged their congregations to maintain a dignity of hope, instilling the lessons of Dr. King along the way: "Faith is taking the first step even when you don't see the whole staircase."

8

Sacrifice Required

Human progress is neither automatic nor inevitable ... every step toward the goal of justice requires sacrifice, suffering, and struggle; the tireless exertions and passionate concern of dedicated individuals.

Dr. Martin Luther King

There can little doubt that the Civil Rights movement of the 1950s and '60s positively impacted most black U.S. citizens across the country. The passing of the Civil Rights Act of 1964 outlawed employment discrimination based on race, color, religion, sex, or national origin. The act also legally abolished segregation. The Voting Rights Act of 1965 addressed and ended racially discriminatory practices such as poll taxes and literacy tests. These legislative changes encouraged societal changes.

By the end of the 1960s, income, home ownership, college enrollment, and life expectancy percentages for black citizens had all risen. As we entered the 1970s, additional positive improvements awaited African Americans. According to a study from the Brookings institute, from 1970–1990, the percentage of black college professors nationwide doubled, as did the number of black physicians during this same time period. Nevertheless, despite these professional and educational advancements, average black household income in 2020 is still only 60 percent of white households. This figure has barely changed since the late 1960s.

The Brookings study also revealed societal improvements. In 1958, 44 percent of white families surveyed declared they would immediately relocate if a black family moved next door. By 1998, that figure plummeted well into single digits. In 1964, only 18 percent of white Americans claimed at least one black friend. By 1998, that percentage rose sharply to a lofty 86 percent. Conversely, when black Americans were asked the same question in 1998, a nearly identical number—87 percent—claimed at least one white friend. Substantial racial progress has also occurred in politics.

In 1991, following an acrimonious Senate debate, Clarence Thomas became only the second African American confirmed for a lifetime appointment to the U.S. Supreme Court. Thomas, a Yale Law School graduate, had previously worked in the office of U.S. Senator John Danforth. He also served the EEOC and assistant secretary of Civil Rights in the Department of Education. Thomas was nominated to the court by President George H. W. Bush. The U.S. Senate confirmed his appointment despite an intense investigation of sexual harassment allegations by a former colleague. As of this writing, Thomas holds the longest tenure of all current justices, and is the only black member on the U.S. Supreme Court.

The most noteworthy, and highest-profile example of political progress occurred in 2008 when the American people elected its first black president. Barack Obama, a Democratic junior senator from Illinois whom few people outside of his home state were familiar with only a couple years prior, outfoxed several seasoned, veteran politicians, including Senator and former First Lady Hillary Clinton, to secure the Democratic nomination. Obama then defeated popular Republican Arizona Senator John McCain for a historic presidential election victory. Four years later, Obama defeated former Republican Massachusetts Governor Mitt Romney to win re-election. Political progress among black citizens was not, however, limited to the Obama presidency.

The 87th U.S. Congress of 1961–62 represented almost no diversity. Only four black officials and one Native American were the only non-white representatives among the 437 members of that particular House of Representatives. The U.S. Senate had zero black representatives and only one Hispanic and one Native American representatives. Fast forward to our current 116th Congress of 2019–20. Substantial progress is evident. The current House of Representatives includes fifty-two black, forty-three Hispanic, fourteen Asian American, and four Native American members. Three black, five Hispanic, and three Asian American representatives are among our 100 U.S. Senators. As we compare figures, and break down percentages, we discover that over one quarter of the House, 25.9 percent to be exact, is non-white, and 11 percent of the Senate is a minority race. However, the latest 2020 U.S. Census estimates project as much as 60 percent of the nation is non-white, which illustrates that a clear inequality still exists among our nation's political power structure.

Although steady progress has occurred in national elections, it is intriguing to note that similar racial progress is not often found at the state levels. In

2020, we have zero black governors leading an individual state. In fact, only four black governors have ever been elected in our entire history. Signs of racial inequality are also evident in several other key areas.

First, black unemployment has actually increased since the peak of the Civil Rights movement. In 1968, the national black unemployment rate was 6.7 percent. In 2017, that figure was 7.5 percent. Poverty rates among black Americans have dropped substantially during that same period, from 34.7 percent in 1968 to 21.4 percent in 2017. However, black poverty rate still pales in comparison to white rates, which were measured at 10 percent in 1968, and 8.8 percent in 2017.

Perhaps the most disturbing trend among black Americans have been increased rates of incarceration, especially for black males. Nationwide incarceration rates for black Americans have tripled since the late 1960s. A black citizen is six times more likely to be slammed into a jail cell than a white citizen. In the State of Indiana, black Americans represent just slightly over 9 percent of the general population, but 34 percent of the prison population. Determining the cause and potential solution to this problem has been a hot political issue in recent years and continues to divide the American public.

Another racial discrepancy to note is the rate of CEOs of major U.S. corporations. As of this writing, only three Fortune 500 companies could claim an African American as their CEO: Marvin Ellison of Lowe's, Kenneth Frazier from Merck, and Roger Ferguson of TIAA. No black females lead Fortune 500 companies.

Affirmative Action developed from the height of the Civil Rights movement. It was first suggested by President John F. Kennedy, later articulated by Lyndon B. Johnson, then expanded by Richard Nixon. An unabashedly political issue, the main objective behind Affirmative Action was to strongly urge potential employers and colleges to grant legitimate consideration to qualified black applicants. The initiative was later expanded to include other minority groups, as well as women, in an effort to ensure equal opportunity for all. Despite honorable intentions, and the ability to grant fair opportunities for various minority groups, Affirmative Action has not been a flawless program. Several notable inconsistencies have caused controversy since its inception.

Some Americans have charged that Affirmative Action has led to reverse discrimination. Multiple charges of this phenomenon have been decided by the courts. One of the most significant reverse discrimination arguments was the case of University of California Regents *v.* Bakke, which was heard by the U.S. Supreme Court. In an effort to ensure more diversity in their medical program, Alan Bakke, despite sterling qualifications, was passed over for several minority candidates. These candidates, it was argued, were less qualified than Bakke. Furthermore, his attorneys argued these racial quotas violated the equal protection clause found in the 14th Amendment of the U.S. Constitution. The U.S. Supreme Court ruled, on June 28, 1978, upheld Affirmative Action policy. Institutions of higher learning were allowed to use a person's race as a factor in determining college admissions. However, the court also ruled that racial quotas were not permissible in the admissions process, therefore did violate the Equal Protection clause. In the forty-plus years since the Bakke case was decided, multiple court cases have challenged Affirmative Action. It continues to be a divisive issue today. Some continue to argue that such a policy leads to reverse discrimination, and excludes qualified white candidates in higher education, and in the workplace. Others argue that Affirmative Action is a necessary tool used to legally ensure that various minority groups are allowed a fair and equal opportunity to pursue the American dream. It is clear that Affirmative Action, although imperfect, is a robust branch that grew from the Civil Rights movement tree and continues to sprout new branches of opportunity for all minority races.

One of the more prominent African American success stories born from new opportunities to develop from Fort Wayne is Eugene Parker. A star athlete, and student, Parker graduated from Concordia High School, and accepted a full ride athletic scholarship to play college basketball at Purdue University. A four-year starter who scored 1,430 career points, Parker excelled enough at the Big-10 school to attract the attention of several NBA scouts. He was picked in the fifth round of the 1978 NBA draft by the San Antonio Spurs. However, playing basketball professionally was not Parker's primary career goal. He wanted to become a lawyer. Parker was accepted into Valparaiso Law school, graduating in 1982.

Shortly after graduating from law school, Parker blended his new degree with his love of sports, fueling a desire to become a sports agent. His first client was fellow Fort Wayne athlete, and Purdue graduate, Roosevelt Barnes, hired under his first agency, Parker & Associates. Following a brief NFL career with the Detroit Lions, Parker groomed Barnes, and fellow Valparaiso Law School classmate Craig McKenzie to begin what would become one of the nation's leading sports agencies representing primarily NFL players.

One of Parker's first major clients was yet another Fort Wayne/Purdue athlete—All-American defensive back Rod Woodson. After getting selected by the Pittsburgh Steelers in the first round of the 1987 NFL draft, Woodson would become Parker's first marquee client. He represented Woodson, a perennial All-Pro, throughout his Hall of Fame career with the Steelers, San Francisco 49ers, Baltimore Ravens, and Oakland Raiders. It was Woodson's stardom that paved the way for Parker's budding empire. Under his newly branded agency Maximum Sports Management, Parker developed a reputation as a personable man of integrity who was also a tough negotiator.

This appealing blend of attributes allowed Parker's agency to prosper with a bevy of future All-Pro caliber NFL players.

Following the Woodson signing, Parker inked two more future NFL Hall of Famers in the next few years who would represent cornerstones for the Dallas Cowboy's dynasty of the 1990s that won three Super Bowls. One was wildly charismatic defensive back Deion "Prime Time" Sanders from Florida State. The other was future NFL all-time rushing leader Emmitt Smith from Florida.

Sanders began his career with the Atlanta Falcons, then played one Super Bowl winning season with the San Francisco 49ers in 1994. After filing for free agency, Parker negotiated in 1995 what was at the time, the richest contract in NFL history for a defensive player. Sanders signed a seven-year deal with the Dallas Cowboys for $35 million with a $13 million signing bonus. Sanders would play most of his remaining years in a Cowboys uniform under the lucrative deal that Parker secured. Sanders was elected to the Pro Football Hall of Fame in 2011. His agent, and friend, delivered his induction speech.

Emmitt Smith played the majority of his NFL career with the Cowboys. One of the most productive and durable running backs in history, Smith starred for all three 1990s Cowboys Super Bowl title winning teams, eclipsing 1,000 yards rushing for an NFL records eleven consecutive seasons. In 1999, Smith passed Walter Payton to become the NFL's all-time rushing leader, a record that he still owns more than twenty years later. Smith was elected to the Pro Football Hall of Fame in 2010.

In addition to marquee stars like Woodson, Sanders, and Smith, Parker consistently added a multitude of NFL All-Pro talent to the Maximum Sports Management portfolio. Larry Fitzgerald, Hines Ward, Derrick Brooks, Devin Hester, Dez Bryant, and future Hall of Famer Curtis Martin represented just a few of the additional superstars that proudly called Parker their agent. Often working behind the scenes based in his Fort Wayne office with little fanfare, Parker preferred to allow his clients, the professional athletes, monopolize the spotlight.

Merging with another agency in 2012, and becoming CEO of Relativity Football, Parker continued to operate as one of the most respected agents in the NFL, possibly heading toward the sports agents Mt. Rushmore. In 2005, *Black Enterprise* magazine ranked him among the fifty most influential blacks in all of sports. He continued to amass substantial wealth for his clients, and himself, until he received shocking news in late 2015—Parker had been diagnosed with advanced kidney cancer. He died four months later. Eugene Parker passed away at the age of sixty in his hometown on March 31, 2016. Surviving were his wife June and their five children. Upon learning of his passing, Sanders said the following: "He taught me manhood without doing it intentionally, and he taught me about the Lord without judging me ... we had true chemistry, love, respect, and admiration." Jovan Barnes, son of Parker's first client Roosevelt Barnes, and certified NFLPA contract adviser with Independent Sports and Entertainment (ISE), said: "Eugene Parker was a great mentor to me, and a great partner to my father. A true trailblazer for future black contract advisers."

Numerous success stories similar to Parker permeate the nation thanks to the efforts of 1950s and 1960s Civil Rights leaders like Martin Luther King. They paved the highway for minority progress to travel effectively through peaceful marches, sit-ins, and other acts of civil disobedience that dominated the era. Some non-minority Americans embraced and supported this progress. Other groups opposed such progress, either through direct means, or use of subtlety.

9

The Language of
the Unheard

The 1980s through present day is often considered the post-Civil Rights era. Segregation was outlawed more than a half century ago. Blatant acts of voter suppression such as literacy tests and poll taxes were eliminated through the Civil Rights Act and Voting Rights Act in the mid-1960s. Affirmative Action policies have encouraged schools of higher learning, and potential employers to objectively consider minority candidates or face legal repercussions from the EEOC, private attorneys, and various government agencies. Statistically speaking, the overall quality of life for blacks has steadily improved over the past four decades. The racial equality highway continues to generate a steady stream of travelers who dream of landing in Dr. King's promised land. Nevertheless, bigotry should not be considered a past tense term. Millions of black Americans have learned that progressive legislation and reform alone cannot change the hearts of some people or eliminate generations of racial oppression. Examples of racism continues to tap the brakes on racial progress. In several high-profile videotaped situations, the brakes were slammed.

Racial Profiling

Darren Martin, a former White House aide to President Obama, was confronted by a half-dozen New York City Police officers while moving into his own Manhattan apartment during an April 2018 evening under suspicion of a burglary in process. Neighborhood bystanders called 911 insisting they had observed Mr. Martin and his associates carrying weapons.

Police questioned Martin, asked for ID, and surveyed his fifth floor apartment before determining that Mr. Martin was not engaged in a crime. Martin was not armed. Much of the exchange was captured on video. A frustrated Martin later Tweeted the following on his social media page: "… call the police on this black man who DEFINITELY doesn't live here. The man who worked for President Obama, and now serves his fellow New Yorkers…. I gotta say, moving up a 5th floor walk up is tough, but each of those 100 plus steps become increasingly grueling with the thought that you're feared or just not wanted in the building." He followed the last Tweet with "#MovingWhileBlack."

During a May 2020 verbal dispute with Amy Cooper, a white female dog owner visiting Central Park, a 911 call was placed falsely accusing unarmed African American bird enthusiast Christian Cooper of assaulting her, even though they were standing approximately 50 feet apart. Ms. Cooper was fired from her job at Franklin Templeton after the video went viral. Much of the exchange was captured on video. Mr. Cooper was not armed.

In March 2019, college student Zayd Atkinson was questioned and detained by a police officer while picking up trash outside his own apartment building. The officer repeatedly asked Mr. Atkinson for identification and to state his apartment number. Mr. Atkinson refused citing the fact that he was a law-abiding college student who had committed no crime. Much of the exchange was captured on video. The Boulder police department later determined that their officer did not have probable cause to detain Mr. Atkinson after the video went viral. The officer resigned and Atkinson later received a $125,000 settlement from the city. Mr. Atkinson was not armed.

These situations represent a small sample of racial profiling, the process of suspecting someone is committing a crime based solely on a person's race. Racial profiling is not limited to interactions with police officers. As we find in two of the previously mentioned situations, sometimes uncomfortable and biased private white citizens can and do initiate and escalate racial profiling. It has long been a disturbing fact of life in America for minority races, not just black Americans. Citizens of Middle Eastern descent have been profiled as suspected terrorists, especially after the suicide airline attacks in New York and Washington, D.C., on September 11, 2001 that killed nearly 3,000 people. Mexicans have been wrongly targeted as members of drug cartels. During the World War II era, law-abiding Japanese-American citizens were profiled to the point that they were forcibly removed from their homes and placed in internment camps following the surprise attack on an American Naval base at Pearl Harbor Hawaii during the "day of infamy," December 7, 1941. Most Japanese American families were not released until the Allies secured victory over the Axis powers in 1945. This practice, as minority races will attest to, is an ongoing struggle in our heavily diverse nation.

Redlining

Another example of racism that has impacted communities of color is redlining. Beginning during the 1930s, lending institutions were reluctant to lend money in low-income, predominantly black neighborhoods. City maps were often outlined with thick red lines in neighborhoods that were unlikely to be approved to loans. This practice was especially prominent in cities with large black populations such as Chicago, Atlanta, and Detroit to name a few. Fort Wayne was not immune to this practice. As a result, low-income minority families faced financial obstacles that were nearly insurmountable.

The Fair Housing Act of 1968 outlawed redlining. This law banned the denial of loans based solely on a person's race, or the raising of interest rates to exorbitant amounts. Furthermore, the Community Reinvestment Act of 1977 required lenders to track loans that were denied in low income areas in order to ensure compliance the Fair Housing Act. Although illegal, some argue that the practice has not disappeared entirely.

Racial Hatred (Charlottesville/SC Church/Trump)

November 8, 2016, Election Day: it is a date that many racially progressive Americans identify as the beginning of a disturbing racial rollback. Donald Trump was elected the forty-fifth president of the United States.

The election to the highest office in the land and the most powerful elected position in the world of an individual with a long history of inflammatory and racially charged remarks and practices troubled African Americans and other minority groups. Conversely, groups of white citizens who opposed the trend of minority groups increasing their power and influence in America pounced on the opportunity to proudly voice their opposition while supporting a Trump-inspired rollback to previous eras of racial imbalance. One such clash between these groups occurred in Charlottesville, Virginia, in 2017.

In February 2017, the Charlottesville city council voted in favor of rechristening two parks previously named for Confederate generals. The proposal also called for the removal of a Robert E. Lee statue. These decisions were met with resistance from a number of Charlottesville residents, including one group that sued the city in an effort to block the changes.

In May 2017, tensions in Charlottesville escalated when white supremacy protestors clashed with counter protestors representing the Black Lives Matter Civil Rights group. Three arrests were made, and one police officer was injured. In July, fifty members of the Ku Klux Klan made an appearance, in full white robes. Counter protestors outnumbered Klansmen by an estimated twenty to one ratio. Shouts of "Racists go home" clashed with "White Power" chants. Police shot pepper spray and tear gas to disperse crowds that were becoming confrontational. Twenty-two arrests were made.

During the evening of August 11, 2017, a white male group of about 250 known as "Unite the Right" wielded Tiki torches, and marched into Emancipation Park, previously known as Lee Park, preceding a rally planned for the following day. Members of various white nationalist groups, including the KKK, neo-Nazi, and pro-Confederacy groups also entered the park, chanting "White lives matter" and "Jews will not replace us" as they marched toward a statue of Thomas Jefferson on the University of Virginia campus. Protestors and counter-protestors clashed again. Dozens of fights broke out near the Jefferson statue, causing the police to break up both demonstrations and declare the protests unlawful.

Violence erupted again the following day. Both groups launched pepper spray at each other. Several additional physical encounters were documented. Virginia Governor Terry McAuliffe declared a state of emergency. "Go home," he told the right-wing extremist groups. "You are not wanted in this great commonwealth. Shame on you."

By 1 p.m., the police had restored order at Emancipation Park, but fights continued to erupt in the streets. "Blood and soil," a common Nazi rallying cry, was consistently chanted by Unite the Right groups, many who waved Confederate and Nazi flags and wore "Make America Great Again" Trump supporter red hats. Chants such as "Nazi scum off our streets" and "punch a Nazi in the mouth" were heard from counter-protestors. Since the state of Virginia has open carry laws, some protestors and counter-protestors were heavily armed, including some individuals that carried semi-automatic weapons. Police in full riot gear continued their work to maintain order amid escalating tensions. By 1:30 p.m., a man later identified as James Fields suddenly revved the engine to his Dodge Charger and deliberately accelerated toward a group of counter-protestors near the intersection of Water and 4th Streets. Bodies were catapulted into the air. Bones crackled and blood gushed on to the street. One woman, thirty-two-year-old Heather Heyer, was killed and fifteen others were injured, some seriously, after the pro-Nazi white nationalist rammed into the crowd. Fields eluded police briefly before being captured and imprisoned. Fields was later convicted of first-degree murder, hit and run, and eight counts of malicious wounding. He was sentenced to two life sentences without the possibility of parole and is currently being held in the West Virginia state penitentiary.

Following the unrest and subsequent tragedy that occurred in Charlottesville, President Trump was asked for his remarks. During his first statement, he referred to "very fine people, on both sides," a comment that angered millions of Americans who interpreted the president's remarks as approval of violent white supremacy. Members of Congress from both political parties also expressed outrage at the president's remarks. Republican Speaker of the House Paul Ryan said of Trump's statements: "It was not only morally ambiguous, it was equivocating."

On June 17, 2015, a twenty-one-year-old white man named Dylan Roof entered the Emanuel AME church in Charleston, South Carolina, one of the oldest black churches in America with a proud Civil Rights history. He was welcomed by a predominantly black congregation to join them for Bible study. After participating in Bible study with thirteen church members, Roof suddenly stood and pulled out a .45-caliber Glock pistol. He began shooting the same parishioners who welcomed him into their place of worship for a study of scripture. Nine people were killed. While protecting her granddaughter crouched below a pew, Felicia Sanders recalled her son Tywanza Sanders pleading with Roof. He asked why he was shooting innocent people. "I have to do this because y'all raping our women and taking over the world," responded Roof who then shot and killed the twenty-six-year-old devout Christian. Felicia Sanders recalled: "I watched my son come into this world, and I watched my son leave this world."

Roof intended to take his own life after completing the massacre, but as he turned the pistol to his head and clicked the trigger, he realized that he had run out of ammo. Roof then dropped the gun, shouted several racial epithets, exited the church, and drove away. He was captured during a traffic stop in Shelby, North Carolina, the following day. Names and addresses of several black churches, a Confederate flag, and empty ammunition boxes were among the belongings retrieved from Roof's car.

Roof plead guilty to his crimes. He chose to represent himself during the sentencing phase of the trial, claiming that his sentence was irrelevant. Roof believed that white nationalists would help free him from prison after successfully winning a nationwide race war. Roof was sentenced to death on January 10, 2017. The U.S. Justice Department reports that this is the first time that the death penalty has been issued for a hate crime. White nationalists have yet to free Roof from his prison cell.

Police Shootings

Questions about unfair treatment for African Americans in the U.S. Justice system continue to persist today. In recent years, several high-profile events have energized and polarized the nation in the area of race relations as it pertains to equal justice.

Trayvon Martin was a lanky seventeen-year old high school student with an easy smile who loved sports and rap music. A Miami resident,

Martin was living temporarily with his father and fiancée in their Sanford, Florida home. During the evening of February 26, 2012, Martin and friends were home playing video games while his father and fiancée were eating dinner at a nearby restaurant. Upon taking a break from games, Martin walked through the Twin Lakes neighborhood toward a 7-11 store where he purchased candy and flavored iced tea. During his return walk to his father's home, Martin was spotted by George Zimmerman, a member of the Twin Lakes volunteer neighborhood watch. Martin, who was unfamiliar to Zimmerman, was wearing a sweatshirt hoodie that was pulled over the top of his head. He was speaking to his girlfriend on his cell phone while he walked. Zimmerman began to follow Martin.

As he began his pursuit, Zimmerman called 911 to report a "suspicious person." He relayed to the dispatcher that Martin "looks like he's up to no good, or he's on drugs or something. It's raining, and he's just walking around." During the conversation with the 911 agent, Zimmerman was instructed not to follow Martin. Zimmerman ignored the request. Martin, now aware of the pursuit, turned around and confronted Zimmerman. "Why are you following me" can be heard during the cell phone call with his girlfriend. A scuffle ensued. Someone is heard yelling "help!," but it is unclear who yelled. During the scuffle, Zimmerman pulled out his 9-mm pistol, and fired a bullet into Martin's chest. Sanford police arrived shortly after the shooting. The teenager was pronounced dead at the scene. Trayvon Martin was not armed.

When questioned by police, Zimmerman claimed the shooting was self-defense. Multiple bruises and a broken nose that Zimmerman inherited during the struggle were observed by officers. The self-defense explanation, under the Florida "stand your ground" law, was accepted. Zimmerman was not initially charged with a crime.

Several segments of the American population were outraged by both the events in Sanford. Following intense public pressure, charges were eventually filed against George Zimmerman. Nearly two months after the confrontation, Zimmerman was charged with second-degree murder.

In June 2013, more than one year after the fatal shooting, the Zimmerman trial began. A six-woman jury panel was selected. On July 13, 2013, a verdict was rendered. Zimmerman was found not guilty of second-degree murder or manslaughter. The self-defense argument convinced the jury that Zimmerman acted appropriately. Demonstrations were held in multiple cities following the not guilty decision. Also, a new Civil Rights movement was launched, perhaps inadvertently, as "#blacklivesmatter" appeared on social media for the first time.

A few days after the Zimmerman verdict was read, President Barack Obama addressed the contentious issue of racial profiling:

You know, when Trayvon Martin was first shot, I said that this could have been my son. Another way of saying that is Trayvon Martin could have been me 35 years ago. And when you think about why, in the African American community at least, there's a lot of pain around what happened here, I think it's important to recognize that the African American community is looking at this issue through a set of experiences and a history that doesn't go away. There are very few African American men who haven't had the experience of being followed when they were shopping in a department store. That includes me. There are very few African American men who haven't had the experience of walking across the street and hearing the locks click on the doors of cars. That happened to me—at least before I was a senator. There are very few African Americans who haven't had the experience of getting on an elevator and a woman clutching her purse nervously and holding her breath until she had a chance to get off. That happens often. And I don't want to exaggerate this, but those sets of experiences inform how the African American community interprets what happened one night in Florida.

Later in the press conference, President Obama suggested a thorough review of racial profiling and Florida's "stand your ground" laws. He also urged Americans do some "soul searching" and conduct open, productive conversations about race.

On August 9, 2014, recent high school graduate Michael Brown and a friend were walking in the middle of a Ferguson, Missouri, street shortly after exiting a nearby convenience store. Darren Wilson of the Ferguson police department confronted the two young men and asked them to move to the sidewalk. Heated words were soon exchanged, and a physical confrontation ensued. Officer Wilson later claimed that Brown initiated the confrontation and reached for his gun. Brown's friend, Dorian Johnson, insisted that Officer Wilson clutched Brown by the neck, initiating the altercation. While the two men struggled, Wilson grabbed and then discharged his weapon, killing Brown instantly. Michael Brown was not armed.

After the shooting, Brown's dead body lie in the middle of the street, surrounded by a pool of blood, in August heat, for over four hours. Angered residents erupted in protests that evening, beginning a period of unrest that would escalate into rioting and looting that lasted for over two weeks.

Two days after the fatal police shooting, an FBI investigation revealed two eyewitnesses who insisted that Brown had his hands raised over his head while Officer Wilson repeatedly shot him. The investigation also revealed security camera footage from the convenience store where Brown and his friend had visited prior to the shooting that indicated an apparent shoplifting incident. Once released to the public, this additional information contributed to an escalation in civil unrest on the streets of Ferguson.

As fall arrived, peace was briefly restored in Ferguson. That peace was interrupted again in late November 2014 when a grand jury chose not to indict Wilson for the fatal shooting of Brown. Violence returned to the streets of the St. Louis suburb. Some 1,500 National Guard troops were called in by the Governor Jay Nixon to maintain order. President Obama felt compelled to address the Ferguson unrest. Speaking directly to Ferguson residents, Obama declared that he had "no sympathy at all for destroying your own communities." Obama then acknowledged frustrations felt by citizens of color in cases of perceived injustice:

> The frustrations that we've seen are not just about a particular incident. They have deep roots in many communities of color who have a sense that our laws are not always being enforced uniformly or fairly. That may not be true everywhere and it's certainly not true for the vast majority of law enforcement officials, but that's an impression that folks have, and it's not just made up—it's rooted in realities that have existed in this country for a long time.

Continuing, Obama again addressed the ongoing rioting in Ferguson:

> There are productive ways of responding and expressing those frustrations, and there are destructive ways of responding. Burning buildings, torching cars, destroying property, putting people at risk—that's destructive, and there's no excuse for it. Those are criminal acts. And people should be prosecuted if they engage in criminal acts.

Once the rioting finished, nearly 300 arrests were made during the two phases of Ferguson rioting. Dozens of buildings were burned. Vandalism and looting caused nearly $5 million in property damage in this city of just over 20,000 located near the St. Louis airport. Reflecting five years later, local activist Kayla Reed had this to say about progress in Ferguson: "I think five years is not a long time. Five years after the Voting Rights Act everything wasn't cured. Five years after the end of slavery, everything wasn't better. And so it's just a marker of time that shows that we've been in this work for five years. But I think that work is still happening."

It was a sweltering hot day in Staten Island, New York, July 17, 2014. Eric Garner, a black man of 6 feet 2 inches, weighing in excess of 300 pounds, was spotted selling cigarettes by local law enforcement. Garner had been previously questioned about selling merchandise without paying taxes on the sale. Several officers confronted Garner, who expressed frustration with frequent police encounters. Officers then wrestled Garner to the ground in an effort to apprehend him. One officer, Daniel Pantaleo, rammed his nightstick around Garner's neck in a chokehold maneuver, a controversial police tactic that had been prohibited by the department since the 1990s. The chokehold cut off oxygen to Garner's windpipe. Multiple witnesses heard Garner gasp "I can't breathe" on multiple occasions. Within minutes, he was dead. Eric Garner was not armed.

Reverend Al Sharpton led a eulogy for Garner days later, followed by a march with an estimated crowd of 2,500 to the very spot where Garner lost his life. Protests followed in Staten Island, but unlike Ferguson they were peaceful.

In December 2014, a grand jury decided not to indict the officers in the Garner matter. After the decision, President Obama said the following:

> Some of you may have heard that there was a decision that came out today by a grand jury not to indict police officers who had interacted with an individual named Eric Garner in New York City, all of which was caught on videotape and speaks to the larger issues that we've been talking about for the last week, the last year, and sadly, for decades, and that is the concern on the part of too many minority communities that law enforcement is not working with them and dealing with them in a fair way … when I met with folks both from Ferguson and law enforcement and clergy and civil rights activists, I said this is an issue that we've been dealing with for too long, and it's time for us to make more progress than we've made. And I'm not interested in talk; I'm interested in action. And I am absolutely committed as President of the United States to making sure that we have a country in which everybody believes in the core principle that we are equal under the law.

Garner's "I can't breathe" has often become a frequent Civil Rights rallying cry used in conjunction with the Black Lives Matter movement. Following a series of lengthy court battles, Pantaleo was terminated from the NYPD in August 2019. He was never found criminally responsible for Garner's death.

Ahmaud Arbery was a twenty-five-year-old former high school football star temporarily living with his mother in Brunswick, Georgia. Arbery dreamed of becoming an electrician like his uncles. He was enrolled in South Georgia Technical College for the fall of 2020 semester. The young man known by family and friends for his fun loving, easy smile enjoyed running to stay in shape. On February 23, 2020, Arbery left home for an early afternoon run. He would never return.

Arbery frequently navigated the nearby Satilla Shores subdivision during his runs. On this particular journey, Arbery was spotted by resident Travis McMichael. Concerned about a series of break-ins in their neighborhood and believing they had witnessed Arbery enter a neighborhood home under construction, McMichael and his father Greg, a retired police officer, hopped in their pickup truck and began pursuing Arbery as a suspect. Both McMichael's carried loaded weapons in their truck during the pursuit. They failed to call 911.

William "Roddie" Bryan, a neighbor of the McMichael's, joined the chase and began filming the event. As they caught up to Arbery, both Bryan and the McMichael's attempted to block his path with their vehicles. Arbery easily dodged both trucks like a nimble halfback avoiding defenders even though Bryan struck Arbery with his truck as he passed. After Arbery eluded them, Travis McMichael quickly exited his vehicle, with loaded shotgun in hand, to confront Arbery. A physical confrontation followed. Presumably out of fear for his own safety, Arbery punched the younger McMichael in the head. McMichael aimed his shotgun and fired three bullets toward Arbery from point-blank range. The last shot caused Arbery to stumble and fall face first, dead, into the street. In the video, McMichael casually turns around and heads toward his truck, leaving the body behind. Ahmaud Arbery was not armed.

Few Americans outside of Glynn County Georgia were made aware of this fatal altercation for more than two months. No charges were filed against any of the three men who aggressively chased Arbery. On May 5, 2020, a local attorney commandeered and submitted the Bryan videotape of the shooting to WGIG, a Brunswick, Georgia, based radio station. The video, which was posted on the station's YouTube channel, soon went viral, shocking millions of Americans. Arbery's father called his son's murder a "modern day lynching." Two days later, facing intense public pressure, both Travis and Greg McMichael were arrested. On May 21, Bryan was also arrested. Considering that no arrests were made until seventy-four days after the shooting suggested that racial discrimination might have been a factor in the investigation.

As nationwide interest in the story swelled, new details emerged. First, a security camera confirmed that Arbery had indeed stopped by the house under construction shortly before running past the McMichael's home. However, Arbery stopped by briefly, according to the homeowner, possibly just to utilize the water source located on the property. The homeowner also noted that multiple individuals, including young children, were shown on camera visiting the property in recent weeks, none with criminal intent or actions. Also, immediately after the shooting, McMichael, according to Bryan, uttered a racial epithet. After researching social media accounts, all three individuals had expressed hateful racist rhetoric on multiple occasions, as well as through text messaging. The McMichael truck also displayed a Confederate flag. As of this writing, the case against Bryan and the McMichael's is pending.

It is early evening Memorial Day, May 25, 2020, in Minneapolis, Minnesota. George Floyd has purchased cigarettes from a convenience store in the Powerderhorn Park section of Minneapolis, Minnesota. Believing the $20 bill passed by Floyd is counterfeit, the store clerk calls the police. When police arrived, they confronted Floyd, plus his two passengers, inside his SUV. Floyd was ordered out of the vehicle. Following some mild resistance, Floyd complied and was walked to the opposite side of the street. Two additional officers arrive on the scene, led by veteran Derek Chauvin, who assumed command of the situation. Floyd was moved to the inside of a squad car, but he complained to officers that he suffered from anxiety and claustrophobia. Floyd offered to instead lay on the ground. The officers complied with the forty-six-year-old suspect's request. Floyd was lowered face down on the ground beside the patrol car.

Fearing that he would resist, Chauvin and two other officers restrain Floyd on the ground. Chauvin kneels directly on Floyd's neck. As Chauvin continues to apply pressure, Floyd complains repeatedly of breathing difficulty. Several bystanders notice Floyd's struggle, and plead with officers to ease the intense pressure. Chauvin refuses. Cries of "I can't breathe" and "please don't kill me" can be heard from Floyd. Chauvin continues to kneel on his neck. Bystanders become more agitated, demanding that officers engage in more humane treatment of the suspect. Chauvin continues to kneel on his neck. Floyd cries out "mama." Chauvin continues to kneel on his neck. Eventually, all movement stops. Several bystanders notice, and angrily confront officers with their observations. Chauvin still continues to kneel on his neck. He finally discontinues the application of pressure after eight minutes and forty-six seconds only after medics arrive. Despite life-saving measures as they depart the scene, Floyd is pronounced dead by medical personnel. George Floyd was not armed.

News and video of Floyd's death became an instant national and global news phenomenon. Following viral video evidence of a recent long line of unarmed black men dying in police custody, the death of George Floyd was the last straw. It became the fuel that ignited enraged protestors by hundreds of thousands around the nation, and eventually around the globe. Protestors staged demonstrations in nearly every major American city for over one week. Some protests, such as Minneapolis and Washington, D.C., lasted longer. Police officers were the target of their anger. Traffic was blocked. Stores were looted and set ablaze. Windows were smashed. Bottles, rocks, firecrackers, and other objects were thrown at riot police around the nation. Tear gas was deployed and rubber bullets were shot routinely in an attempt to disperse crowds and disengage violent behavior. Mass arrests were made. During multiple protests, police were accused of using excessive force. Ironically, excessive force by police is precisely what led citizens to protest *en masse*.

During the evenings of May 29 and May 30, downtown Fort Wayne also experienced aggressive demonstrations. Clashes with police occurred in fashions similar to other large cities around the nation. Downtown crowds were estimated by some officials to exceed 1,000 demonstrators both evenings. Tear gas and pepper spray were deployed against protestors both evenings after traffic was blocked on Clinton Street in front of the Allen County Courthouse. One protestor was permanently blinded when a tear gas canister hit him directly in one eye. Various projectiles, including firecrackers, were thrown at police officers. During the evening of the 29th, as many as fifty windows were smashed in downtown businesses.

Not since the Civil Rights and anti-Vietnam War protests of the 1960s had America seen such a massive confluence of public discord. Although protests ended in most American cities by mid-June, other cities, such as Portland, Oregon, demonstrations demanding police reform continued.

Some experts have begun to wonder if we are witnessing the beginning of a second Civil Rights movement. Others have wondered what Martin Luther King would think of the wave of George Floyd protests were he alive to witness the transformative events that transfixed a nation. Perhaps the answer lies in these remarks from Dr. King's 1967 speech, which illustrates with compete clarity, disturbing and timeless relevance:

> Let me say as I've always said, and I will always continue to say, that riots are socially destructive, and self-defeating.... But in the final analysis, a riot is the language of the unheard. And what is it that America has failed to hear? It has failed to hear that the plight of the Negro poor has worsened over the last few years. It has failed to hear that the promises of freedom and justice have not been met. And it has failed to hear that large segments of white society are more concerned about tranquility and the status quo than about justice, equality, and humanity. And so, in a real sense our nation's summers of riots are caused by our nation's winters of delays. And as long as America postpones justice, we stand in the position of having these recurrences of violence and riots over and over again.

10

Freedom Demanded

"Freedom is never voluntarily given by the oppressor. It must be demanded by the oppressed." Dr. Martin Luther King made this declaration in "Letter from a Birmingham Jail." The pursuit of absolute, complete freedom for all African Americans was the goal of the Civil Rights movement of the 1950s and 1960s. Pursuit of that unfulfilled goal continues today.

Throughout the '50s and '60s, the Civil Rights movement primarily sought to end all forms of segregation. Securing voting rights, plus ensuring equal professional, educational, and housing opportunities also topped the mission. The movement also sought fair and equal treatment via symbiotic relationships with law enforcement. In 2020, although segregation and some forms of voter suppression have been outlawed for over fifty years, *de facto* segregation still exists. So does voter suppression. Arguments have been proposed that Voter ID requirements and pushback against mail in voting disenfranchises some citizens. The Civil Rights Act outlawed employment discrimination, but evidence suggests that certain candidates are often less likely to receive a phone call for an interview if they have an ethnic, non-white sounding name. Some have suggested that the same issues occur in the housing market, and college admissions. Although there can be little doubt that society has progressed as we strive toward making Martin Luther King's dream a reality, it is also evident that there is still much work to be done. This seems especially true regarding the long, troubled history of a fractured relationship between law enforcement and black male citizens. Throughout the nation, civic and political leaders continue to meet in the wake of global protests following the George Floyd killing in May 2020 to address, and hopefully rectify this longstanding problem that exists in far too many American cities. Ensuring more police transparency is one positive step in that direction. In July 2020, Fort Wayne city council passed an ordinance requiring all city police officers to be equipped with body cameras by 2022.

In other encouraging news, hate crimes in Fort Wayne have been minimal in recent years. According to FBI statistics, only six hate crimes were reported in the city over the past decade, 2010–2019. Although any society should strive for a goal of zero hate crimes, when our appalling history of racism is taken into consideration, both locally and nationally, these figures represent some cause for optimism.

Dr. Martin Luther King's Fort Wayne Visit Revisited: MLK III

Martin Luther King III was only ten years old when his father was assassinated. Shaken by his father's untimely passing, young Martin dedicated his own life to carrying the torch for racial unity and equality. Martin III, who once fulfilled his father's position as the head of the SCLC from 1997–2003, is a popular speaker and community activist who works to enrich his father's legacy. As he explained during a 2005 interview with *Ebony* magazine: "My father's views were unequivocal, and I have found them to be invaluable to me as guidelines for prayerful consideration of current events and issues." In June 2019, Martin III accepted an invitation from Reverend Bill McGill from Imani Baptist Temple to travel to Fort Wayne and speak during the anniversary of his father's visit. Completing his journey to the Summit City to speak to a captive audience proved to be a challenging task.

Thunderstorms pounded Fort Wayne and the surrounding area during the evening of June 5, 2019, causing King's flight to be delayed. At one point, it became necessary to take a helicopter in order to complete his trip. He arrived at the Embassy theater to begin his presentation at 10 p.m.—three hours later than scheduled. Despite the delays, King was greeted by a near capacity, multi-racial crowd in the 2,500-seat auditorium.

King did not immediately depart Fort Wayne. The following morning, Reverend McGill arranged for another important ceremony requiring King's participation—giving another short speech, followed by the laying of a wreath at the foot of the city's Dr. Martin Luther King Jr. memorial bridge. King used the symbolic opportunity of this ceremony to address pertinent newsworthy topics, ironically, many of the same topics that his father consistently fought a half-century earlier. One of those issues was poverty.

"A nation with a multi-trillion dollar economy should not have poverty. At all. That should be unacceptable." Continuing, King also addressed another one of his father's most important Civil Rights issues—racism. "A nation as diverse as these United States of America should really not even have racism. It's all right to promote your own ethnicity. But you don't have to do that and diminish anyone else. That's what racism does. It makes one person feel superior, or one ethnic group, to another."

Dr. Martin Luther King Memorial Bridge

When construction began on the Martin Luther King memorial bridge in 2010, city planners envisioned a bridge that would honor Dr. King while guiding travelers into downtown Fort Wayne. That mission was accomplished. The $8.8 million project was completed, and dedicated June 5, 2012, the anniversary of Dr. King's visit. Dr. Derek King, nephew of Martin Luther King, attended the dedication ceremony. "There are not many municipalities that have dedicated a bridge—and certainly not of this caliber—in the name of Dr. Martin Luther King Jr.," he offered. "Fort Wayne has done something very unique … it's a grand statement into Fort Wayne's downtown and a fine tribute to my uncle."

Some 704 LED lights in rainbow colors and various patterns blaze the night sky every evening, reflecting off the St. Mary's river below. During the daytime, residents enjoy a section of the citywide River Greenway trail beneath the bridge for walking and biking.

The bridge bears a resemblance to the Edmund Pettis bridge in Alabama, site of the violent showdown between police and demonstrators during the march from Selma to Montgomery, Alabama in 1965. This structure has also generated new local Civil Rights memories. In addition to the Martin Luther King III wreath ceremony, the entrance of the bridge was used as a meeting point during Fort Wayne's George Floyd protest demonstrations. This bridge was also used during a city sanctioned Unity march held on June 4, 2020, only days after demonstrators and police violently clashed. That afternoon, hundreds of demonstrators marched from the Allen County Courthouse to the MLK bridge with police officers, and top city officials, including Mayor Tom Henry.

A Permanent Memorial

Nearly three score years after his appearance, Fort Wayne city-council made the decision in early 2020 to forever commemorate Dr. King's lone trip to the Summit City. During a February meeting, council members Michelle Chambers and Russ Jehl proposed launching a committee that would investigate and design a lasting MLK tribute. The proposal passed unanimously. "Martin Luther King is a national hero. I feel that his visit to Fort Wayne should be forever memorialized," declared council woman Chambers. African American civic leaders have been collaborating, as of this writing, with area artists to develop the style and location for this memorial. Chambers said she is hoping for a design that includes modern, interactive technology rather than a simple statue or historical marker.

MLK Club

The MLK Club is committed to championing the legacy of the late Civil Rights leader. Founded in 1985, the Fort Wayne MLK Club chapter holds annual community events during the anniversaries of Dr. King's birthday in January, as well as his death in April. Embarking on annual summer trips to areas of historical significance from the Civil Rights struggle is another benefit that members enjoy. The MLK Club has previously journeyed south to visit the National Civil Rights museum in Memphis, Tennessee. This museum is located on the former grounds of the Lorraine Motel, site of Dr. King's assassination on April 4, 1968. Additional trips have been taken to historical sites in Birmingham, Montgomery, and Selma, Alabama. As stated in the club mission: "We the Fort Wayne Martin Luther King Jr Club support the non-violent philosophy and teachings of Dr. Martin Luther King Jr. When he said that must learn to live together as brothers and sisters, or we will perish together as fools. We believe that 'the time is right to always do what is right.'" MLK Club President Bennie Edwards is hopeful that growth through cultural awareness will continue to enrich Fort Wayne and surrounding communities.

11

The Measure of a Man

During the evening of July 28, 2020, I hosted a roundtable discussion via Zoom conference to discuss the state of race relations in America, both past and present. Current issues such as white privilege, racial profiling, mass incarceration, and Black Lives Matter were discussed. The following is a snapshot summary of that conference. Our panel of participants included:

Joe Adams:	retired/son of Reverend Clyde Adams
Marshall White:	son of Reverend Jesse White, founder/CEO Unity Performing Arts
Denise Porter-Ross:	retired/Union Baptist Church historian
Jahrae Hampton:	social worker, volleyball coach
Khalid Griffin:	educator/pastor
Jovan Barnes:	sports agent—Independent Sports & Entertainment
Darrion White:	entrepreneur/athletic coach
Bennie Edwards:	president, local MLK Club
Pastor Cedric Walker:	pastor Joshua's temple

White Privilege

JOE ADAMS: "Back in the '50s when our family came here [to Fort Wayne], what you call 'white privilege' was racism. That's what it was, plain and simple. They didn't want people of color invading their world. So, we had to open up restaurants, hotels, and movie theaters. Back then [1950s], blacks were not allowed on the main floor of movie theaters. We were only allowed to go up into the balcony. Well, Dad got together with the kids and some of the adults from the church, and we went in, and sat down on the first floor of the Wayne Theater. Dad had our back because he had the Assistant Police Chief with him. If we had any problems, he was there to defend us…. Fort Wayne has come a long way since then…. Civil Rights has not changed, it's just has different people that are involved. But, it's the same discrimination and difficulties that we faced back in the fifties, sixties, and seventies, fighting for jobs, schooling, and education, and that sort of thing."

DENISE PORTER-ROSS: "Part of racism changed over the years to not just the color of your skin, but it changed in economic issues. It changed in housing opportunities. It changed whether or not you could get into a decent school. It changed in whether or not you could run for an elected office. My parents were tennis pros when I was growing up, but tennis was not necessarily a 'black sport.' My father used to play tennis with a white friend who was Mormon at Swinney Park. This friend, who called himself a good Christian, once told my father: 'Jim, it's just too bad you can't get to heaven. God will only let white people into heaven.'

MARSHALL WHITE: "We lived through the heart of the Civil Rights movement. Once we woke up to three crosses burning on our fron lawn…. My Dad and Jesse Jackson best friends. Dad was the Civil Rights leader of this area. He and Jesse Jackson planned boycotts together. We had him over for dinner many times."

KHALID GRIFFIN: "White privilege is unearned assets and resources that whites can use however and whenever they want…. Privilege says I can go for a run in my neighborhood and not be questioned about my motives and intentions. It re-establishes the notion that whites have established what is good, and they don't have to work to benefit from that standard."

DARRION WHITE: "In my world, it seems that white privilege and white supremacy are synonymous. I had an experience while I was in college where me and my Caucasian roommate violated a team rule. We were hanging out together all summer. We both failed our drug test. I was told that I could not resume team activities until I passed the test. He was told: 'just stay off it, son.' He was allowed to practice, and travel with the team, and didn't have to show a negative drug test to come back to the team. That's the definition of white privilege. It's even more prevalent today. For instance, I've heard stories of [white] friends that were pulled over. They were told they could go home, they were able to call parents to get rides, whereas in my experience, I was never given the same opportunities. White privilege to me is the other side of the coin of racism. Racism is the systematic approach to oppression because of their [skin] color. The other side is the advantages given to people that are in the position of power so that they keep it."

KHALID GRIFFIN: "The idea that if I have a college across my chest that I need to do these things to be appear safe, and approachable, the reality is those things are precautions, but no guarantees that we'll remain 100% safe. Uncle Marshall and I live in the same neighborhood. It's one of the more affluent neighborhoods in Fort Wayne. The reality is when we take walks, there are certain things we have to keep in mind. We are not necessarily exempt from being profiled. So, there are parameters we can put in place, but it's still not 100% sure that we'll make it home in one piece, or without any issues at all."

DARRION WHITE: "At recent summer athletic camp [Traction], roundtable discussion with mothers of athletes. Interesting discussion differences between black vs white mothers. Both had kids approaching 16 years old where they were getting ready to drive. The conversation that the black mother had with her son was drastically different that the conversation that the white mother had with her son. The white mother said that she tells her kid to make sure you wear your seat belt, and don't do anything crazy. Real simple. The black mother's conversation was completely different. It started with the same things—make sure you wear your seat belt, and that you abide by the safety laws, but if you get pulled over, make sure you don't reach too quickly for anything, make sure you have your license and registration, don't have anything in the car, don't talk back … a long laundry list of things for him to do. That dichotomy is what illustrates white privilege."

JAE HAMPTON: "I had similar teaching in my house growing up in South Carolina. I was told to dress a certain way, talk a certain way, act a certain way so I won't seem threatening."

Racial Profiling

JAE HAMPTON: "A couple years ago, I was in Minnesota for a volleyball tournament. I'm decked out in all my volleyball gear, and I have a backpack on. Downtown knows about the tournament because you have players and coaches walking all over the place wearing their gear. I end walking into a Walgreens to grab some things. First, apparently a woman thought that I was following her. She gave me a look like she was freaked out. At that same time, as I walked in the door and looked to my right, I see a guy who instantly calls for a security check on this particular aisle. I realized that I was in that aisle. So, I noticed that, and grabbed what I wanted to eat. Security was late because I was already at the register, but I could see this guy throw his hand across his neck to say 'go away.' That's when I knew [that I had been racial profiled]. I kicked myself for not saying anything at the time because I was upset. Everything I was wearing showed that I was a part of volleyball, I'm just getting something to eat, you have people walking in and out of your establishment all day. That was the first time that I was aware of being racially profiled. It may have happened before, but this was the first time it was evident. It was a shocker to me. It sucks that even today, I still have to work a little harder just to make sure I'm viewed as a regular person, and not someone who's put into a category just because I'm an African American male."

JOVAN BARNES: "I work with professional athletes all the time. Racial profiling hits us at all levels, whether it's a regular Joe Shmo, or a professional athlete. When I played, I was with the New York Jets for a short moment. There were times when I was in a fancier, luxury store. I could afford to buy their stuff. I was being followed around, and asked: 'What are you doing here? Do you need something?' I responded that I was just shopping, just looking around, the same as these other [white] folks, and you don't bother them. Just recently, a couple of my clients who just got drafted [by the NFL] were in a luxury condo and were approached on many occasions. They were asked: 'Do you live here? What is your business here?' Other [white] individuals would walk around, and there were no issues. It is frustrating when you can't do the same things that other folks can. You get profiled. You get thought of as a threat. You get thought of as less than, and as a person who is not worthy of enjoying the luxuries in life, or to just be who you are. It's unfortunate that this is still happening in 2020, but it is real."

DENISE PORTER-ROSS: "About ten years ago, my son and two of his buddies were walking one house to other and found out they were in the wrong subdivision. They decided to cut across golf course from

Arlington Park to Cherry Hill. They were looking in back windows of houses to find out where their friend's party was. I told them later, you don't ever go anywhere where you don't know where you're going. I said: 'people will shoot you.' They said: 'But we weren't doing anything wrong!' I told them: 'that's not the point.' These are things you have to teach kids as a mother. You have tears in your eyes as you're doing it, but you know if you don't say these things to them, ain't nothing going to protect them but God."

Mass Incarceration

DARRION WHITE: "The Mass Incarceration problem started with the War on Drugs, then the Clinton's perpetuated the problem. It put a lot of black people in jail for lesser crimes."

KHALID GRIFFIN: "This problem dates back to Reconstruction following the end of the Civil War.... Black were free, but this idea of liberation was challenged quickly because the laws changed. You see things like the Black Codes. While we couldn't work for free anymore like the days of slavery, we will build a system that we call prison, we'll catch you for silly stuff, and we'll get labor out of you that way. It was specifically targeted toward black men. We all know that when you remove the man from the home, the ramifications don't just affect that house. They affect generations to come. Not only is this [racism] systematic, but it was very intentional in response to the Reconstruction period and laws were put in place to make sure that black remained oppressed, and away from their families altogether. It still affects generations today."

DARRION WHITE: "Reconstruction was a period of less than 20 years where the government had programs in place to help black people. But then when that ended, they ushered in the Jim Crow laws.

That's when you start to see mass incarceration in its infancy, plus the beginning of indentured servitude. It also starts in the school system with the school to prison pipeline where they start to condition African American males to be in prison at some point. Many times they're put in classes labeled special-ed when they aren't, which takes them away from certain scholarship [opportunities] that they can't get, and sends them down a certain path for school they shouldn't be on, and in turn this perpetuates prison later on in life. There's a lot of research that's been done on this school to prison pipeline. It has its roots in the Reconstruction period right as Jim Crow was starting."

MARSHALL WHITE: "One of the challenges for our country now are that the past atrocities that we've experienced as a country—mass incarceration, the educational system, Jim Crow, all of these entities were created to keep black in a moderate position where they did not advance. So, when you look at Police, the judicial system, the educational structure, every one of these systems have not changed. We're only looking at the symptoms, such as mass incarceration and police brutality. We don't realize that the symptoms are deeper than what we're seeing. When you hear white people say, "I'm not racist," they might not be racist, but they are all implicitly and complicitly experiencing the benefits of this system that keeps one race up, and another one down. Everything is involved in this process.... We've got work to do, and the work is deep. It's amazing when I meet white people who want to be part of the solution, I applaud them, but the majority of white people will need to give up their way of life, and embrace a whole new way of living if they're going to be a part of this change. You can't continue to benefit from the system that helped white people advance. We almost need to disrupt this entire structure in order to move forward. That's scary to most

DARRION WHITE: [white] people. That's why militias are growing." "Racism is not a black issue. It's a white issue. It needs to be taken care of in white homes, at their dinner tables, talking to their children, in their jobs with what they would call their 'good old boys club'"

Black Lives Matter/All Lives Matter

MARSHALL WHITE: "It's no different than in October when you see the football players, and you see the basketball players, wear pink. They're wearing pink simply because of cancer. They're not saying heart attacks don't matter. They're giving particular attention that season to that particular disease. So that's what the Black Lives Matter movement is about. It's giving the right attention, right now, to the situation that we need to focus on. To say, 'All lives matter' would be equal for me to say to Vera Bradley "diabetes matters!!" I'm actually diluting the whole purpose why they're promoting [fighting] cancer. White people don't realize they're exposing their stupidity when they say that."

KHALID GRIFFIN: "Historically, there has been no value for black lives. The only reason that Ahmaud [Arbery] got the attention that he did after two months was because of the Black Lives Matter movement where people were literally enraged by what happened. The only reason that all four cops were held accountable for the situation with George Floyd was because this country went up in flames, quite literally. But think about all we have to do to fulfill this ideology that Black Lives Matter. The best way I describe it when I'm talking to people, is to add one word—Black Lives Matter, too. I think adding that word really does help people understand it's not devaluing other lives, it's saying we matter too."

DARRION WHITE: "Imagine if you pull into a neighborhood, and there's a house on fire, and a neighbor yells 'hey, all houses matter!!' It's the house that's on fire that needs to be put out now. I know all houses matter. I know they're all important, but this one's on fire. We need to put this fire out.... If you walk by a dog, and it's starving, you feed that dog just because of your humanity. You don't need to have been a dog before. You don't need to experience starving without walking by that starving dog and realize that you need to feed it. You don't need to have experienced racism before in order to help. Empathy is a good place to start."

KHALID GRIFFIN: "Our younger [black] students, high school and college aged, the idea that they matter is a fundamental concept that I don't think they grasp. That's because students are now in classes with students of so many different ethnicities. It's out of sight, out of mind because they don't feel what other individuals like my uncles felt growing up. You had to have a sense of pride of being black because you were reminded every day that you're nothing. So that created a sense of bond and cohesion because society said it's us versus you, and you gonna feel it.... We can't over estimate that value we have for ourselves, particularly for this generation coming up behind us because unless tragic things happen, we're not really having a sense of pride as it relates to being an advocate for our own struggle and passing information down and sharing it amongst ourselves."

DARRION WHITE: "We need to instill in our children to have a sense of pride. Our history didn't start with slavery. Regular schools will tell us that our history started on the boat, on the way here [to America]. They won't tell you what we were doing before we got here. They need to know about African civilizations like Kush. You need to know about Mansa Musa. That's our story. We come from kings and queens. As educators, we know that, but our children need to know that too."

MARSHALL WHITE:	"This is not just a challenge for the white community, but also the black community. The black community is split because you have some black conservatives who are deeply opposed to the Black Lives Matter movement and police brutality because they believe racism doesn't exist. Black people need to be re-educated, because they've been educated wrong, where white people need additional education.... Protesting is beautiful, but preparation is better. Today the church needs to be a place of education, and preparation."
DENISE PORTER-ROSS:	"I was 65 before I realized that Great Britain and the powers of Europe actually came to a meeting, and carved out what they were going to take from Africa while we were just ending our Civil War, and going through Reconstruction. We need to know our history.... We all have got to live here together."
JAHE HAMPTON:	"We have this movement, but barely a month later, we barely hear pieces of it. We hit hard, then it died. How can we make sure they are making an impact so that the conversation can continue? We need to be a village again, to raise our young people. Right now, their understanding is through rap, and the NBA, and other sports figures, and the guys that are telling you to do all the wrong things, saying 'you go after you, boo boo,' whereas we're trying to get you back to understanding that we need each other. We can lean on each other, and we'll be stronger."
KHALID GRIFFIN	[condensed quote from Carter Woodson]: "If you control a person's mind, you don't have to worry about what they'll do. If you convince a person that he's inferior in his mind, if there is no back door, he'll build one, because he'll conclude that he's not worthy to walk through the front door. In many regards, that's where we are as a people. That's why, quite frankly, I stopped using the 'N' word. I used it as a young man, and in college, until something hit one day, and I realized that this oppressive term was

used to keep us down and demean us. Now white people don't have to call us that, because we call each other that, and we act accordingly. And I think that's the epitome of what Carter G. Woodson meant when he said if they can get in your mind, they're hands off at that point, they'll act accordingly, and its mission complete.... If we don't view ourselves beyond the way we're perceived in society, we won't ever pursue anything else."

MARSHALL WHITE: "Most people my age may not see that promised land that Martin Luther King talked about, but I believe this younger generation will see it, and I believe this generation also, if they get theirs heads right, will be able to manage it."

KHALID GRIFFIN: "There are people who view this as a good crisis, and they don't want it to go to waste.... But, when there's no more cameras, and no more headlines, that's when the real work begins."

DARRION WHITE: "Remember when King and Malcolm were starting to move closer together? That's when they wiped them both out. So, we've got to be wiling for some sacrifice too. Because you know when we start doing things, there's some powers that be that don't want to see that. Remember, Malcolm had a religious revelation when he realized that all white people weren't the devil. He went to Mecca, and came back home, and he wanted to do some work with Martin Luther King, and Martin was realizing that maybe all non-violence wasn't the way to go, and he was asking for that check that bounced. So, right when he started talking about that bounced check, and we were going to come and get what we were owed, that's when they wiped them out."

MARSHALL WHITE: "They [King and Malcolm X] possessed something that this generation lacks, which is commitment. We're dedicated to the work, but not committed to the process.... There was a process that King, Malcolm, and the rest of them had to follow in order to have any impact. The mindset of this younger generation is doing

	something, but not being committed to a process to get something done productively. If you don't want to sit down long enough to learn the process, you're not going to last. You're going to quit before you get there. So, I try to challenge these young people to learn the process."
DENISE PORTER-ROSS:	"There were times when Rev. Adams, Rev. White, Rev. Dixie, Rev. Walker and others had to get together themselves in those rooms before they were ready to speak out. That's the process."
REV. WALKER:	"We ought to always look back in order to see how we should move forward…. Our families and the black churches were intimately tied to the Civil Rights movement. That was our greatest mission…. We have seen crosses burned on our yards as kids. There were times schools had to hold classes in the basement, and in educational areas of our churches [due to boycotts]. But the church always stayed together. It was our social center. It can be that way again."
BENNIE EDWARDS:	"Fort Wayne has changed a lot over the last 30–40 years, for the better I would say…. Fort Wayne has a story, and a lot of history. I hope it will come out for the better of our young people. After being a part of the Martin Luther King club for over 30 years, one of the things I want to do is to see the memory and legacy of Dr. King live on here in Fort Wayne as well as throughout the country."
JAHE HAMPTON:	"Just because you come from poverty, doesn't mean you have to stay in poverty. You have to build and find success. Success is not about how many material things you can own, or how much money you have in your back pocket. Success to me is about waking up every day, and deciding if you're happy about what you're doing, and the lives you are connected with, and keeping a smile on your face even during the hard times. Happy always goes up and down, but the joy should never die."

I love America but I am ashamed our country's inability, or willingness, to cure racism. It is a corrosive stain that has never fully washed away. And it is alive and well in 2020. Racism did not end with the 13th Amendment. It did not end with the Civil Rights movement. It did not end with the election of Barack Obama. In recent years, the advent of smartphones has recorded clear-cut cases of racial harassment and brutality. Yet, when the videos go viral, the excuse and justification train chugs along driven by white Americans who do not share Dr. King's dream of racial unity and equality. The expectation for black behavior from these white Americans mirrors the same expectations too often witnessed throughout our history: an expectation of total and complete black obedience to white superiority. If only black citizens would have obediently followed the advice and guidelines from white leadership, there would have been no criticism, no injuries, no loss of life.

What if fourteen-year-old Emmitt Till did not whistle at a white woman? He would not have been tortured and killed by her enraged husband and brother in law.

What if Ahmaud Arbery did not stop for a drink of water at a house under construction? He would not have been killed by two paranoid white neighbors.

What if Eric Garner did not try to sell cigarettes on the black market? He would not have been choked to death by police officers.

What if George Floyd did not try to pass a counterfeit $20 bill? He would not have been choked to death by police officers.

What if Trayvon Martin would not have confronted a stalker? He would not have been killed by self-appointed neighborhood watch officer George Zimmerman.
What if Rodney King would have avoiding doing drugs? He would not have been viciously beaten, almost fatally, by a gang of police officers.

What if Colin Kaepernick would have stood for the National Anthem? He would not have become the most hated athlete in America and lost the prestige and money that comes from playing Quarterback in the NFL.

What if Breonna Taylor did not have an ex-boyfriend with a history of drug dealing? She would not have been murdered in her sleep by police officers.

What if Tommie Smith and John Carlos did not raise their fists during the 1968 Summer Olympics? They would not have become hated athletes who were stripped of their medals, expelled from Olympic village, and received regular death threats.

What if John Lewis would have obediently turned around as instructed on the Edmund Pettis bridge? He would not have been beaten by police officers.

What if The Little Rock 9 would have continued attending an all-black school? They would not have been taunted, spit on, threatened, and physically assaulted by unhinged white mobs.

What if Martin Luther King had obeyed the injunction against parading in Birmingham? He would not have been jailed in solitary confinement.

What if Rosa Parks would have obeyed Jim Crow transportation laws and moved to the back of the bus as instructed? She would not have been arrested.

What if Arthur McDuffie did not run a red light? He would not have been beaten fatally by Police officers.

What if children would have remained in Birmingham schools? They would not have been assaulted with police dogs and fire hoses, and then jailed.

What if college students would not have sat at a whites-only lunch counter? They would not have been physically assaulted by a white mob, then arrested.

What if Civil Rights activists would not have taken freedom rides and respected generations of segregation? Their bus would not have been bombed.

What if Ernest Lacy did not walk into a neighborhood grocery store in Milwaukee and physically resemble a criminal suspect? He would not have died at the hands of city police officers.

What if three young activists had not have traveled to Mississippi in 1964 to register African Americans to vote? They would not have been abducted and murdered by members of the KKK.

Despite our troublesome history of racism, progress has steadily occurred. The late Hana Stith, former curator of Fort Wayne's African American museum, declared in an August 27, 2003 *News-Sentinel* article: "If King could come back and see improvements that have been made, he would be pleased."

If Dr. King were alive today, we can safely assert that he would urge all of us to continue learning from each other. To listen. To empathize. To be kind. To consider other perspectives. Dr. King once claimed: "The measure of a man is not where he stands in moments of comfort and convenience, but where he stands at times of challenge and controversy." We are currently facing one of those moments in America. Hopefully, we as a nation will rise up and meet that challenge.

Bibliography

E-mail Communication

Barnes, Jovan, e-mail communication with author, September 28, 2020
Edwards, Bennie, e-mail communication with author, September 28, 2020
Helmke, Paul, e-mail communication with author, May 15, 2020
Knoblauch, Jennifer, e-mail communication with author, July 10, 2020
Long, Robert, e-mail communication with author, May 14, 2020
McGill, Rev. Bill, e-mail communication with author, May 25, 2020; June 1, 2020
Meister, Greg, e-mail communication with author, May 12, 2020; May 17, 2020, e-mail communication with author, "From Truck to Tent," June 30, 2020
Meister, Peter, e-mail communication with author, May 4, 2020; May 8, 2020; May 18, 2020; June 30, 2020; September 28, 2020
Shawgo, Ron, e-mail communication with author, June 5, 2020

Images

"Dr. King at microphone." *Journal-Gazette,* June 6, 1963, 1A.
Elliott, Chris. "John Nuckols statue." 2020. jpg.
 "Build dikes of courage." MLK bridge Fort Wayne. 2020. jpg.
 "A man cannot ride your back." MLK bridge Fort Wayne. 2020. jpg.
 "Come on different ships." MLK bridge Fort Wayne. 2020. jpg.
 "Hatred paralyzes life." MLK bridge Fort Wayne. 2020. jpg.

"Darkness cannot drive out darkness." MLK bridge Fort Wayne. 2020. jpg.

"Peace is not merely a distant goal." MLK bridge Fort Wayne. 2020. jpg.

"Our loyalties must transcend our race." MLK bridge Fort Wayne. 2020. jpg.

"I refuse to accept the idea." MLK bridge Fort Wayne. 2020. jpg.

"The quality, not the longevity." MLK bridge Fort Wayne. 2020. jpg.

"Injustice anywhere." MLK bridge Fort Wayne. 2020. jpg.

"Our lives begin to end." MLK bridge Fort Wayne. 2020. jpg.

"Faith is taking the first step." MLK bridge Fort Wayne. 2020. jpg.

"Martin Luther King Jr.- Honoring his life and legacy." MLK bridge Fort Wayne. 2020. jpg.

"The time is always right." MLK bridge Fort Wayne. 2020. jpg.

"Right, temporarily defeated." MLK bridge Fort Wayne. 2020. jpg.

"We must learn to live together." MLK bridge Fort Wayne. 2020. jpg.

"I have decided to stick with love." MLK bridge Fort Wayne. 2020. jpg.

"In the end, we will remember." MLK bridge Fort Wayne. 2020. jpg.

"Man must evolve." MLK bridge Fort Wayne. 2020. jpg.

"The ultimate measure of a man." MLK bridge Fort Wayne. 2020. jpg.

"Power at its best." MLK bridge Fort Wayne. 2020. jpg.

"A genuine leader." MLK bridge Fort Wayne. 2020. jpg.

"Landmark for peace memorial." MLK foreground. Indianapolis. 2020. jpg.

"Landmark for peace memorial." RFK foreground. Indianapolis. 2020. jpg.

"Unity Day—officer walks with children." Fort Wayne. 2020. jpg.

"Unity Day---protestors gather at MLK bridge." Fort Wayne. 2020. jpg.

"Unity Day---protestors begin march." Fort Wayne. 2020. jpg.

"Frontiersmen sponsor Dr. King appearance." *Journal-Gazette,* June 6, 1963, 1B.

"Martin Luther King III." 2019. WPTA-21 television, Fort Wayne.

"MLK Club logo." www.mlkclubfw.com/. Accessed September 21, 2020.

"Protest Dr. King appearance." *Journal-Gazette,* June 6, 1963, 1B.

"Seminarians join in protest." *Journal-Gazette,* May 2, 1964.

Studio Sirois. "MLK Bridge-daytime." 2020. jpg.

Studio Sirois. "MLK Bridge-evening." 2020. jpg.

"Theological students and laymen picket Wallace." *Journal-Gazette,* May 2, 1964.

"Urban League Head Here." *Journal-Gazette,* February 28, 1963.

Interviews

Adams, Joseph, telephone interview, July 11, 2020; July 17, 2020; August 31, 2020

Chambers, Michelle, telephone interview, May 8, 2020

Helmke, Paul, Zoom interview, April 29, 2020

Kelsaw, Richard, telephone interview, July 17, 2020
Long, Robert, telephone interview, May 6, 2020
Meister, Greg, telephone interview, May 11, 2020
Meister, Peter, Zoom interview, May 4, 2020
Noack, Kaye Ann, telephone interview, May 18, 2020
Porter-Ross, Denise, telephone interview, July 10, 2020
White, Marshall, Zoom conference interview, July 16, 2020; September 27, 2020

Online

"16th street Baptist church bombing," www.nps.gov/articles/16thstreetbaptist. htm, accessed July 9, 2020.

"7th Circuit upholds Fort Wayne and Indiana laws which prohibit insurance redlining," fairhousing.com/news-archive/advocate/1994/7th-circuit- upholds-fort-wane-indiana-laws-which-prohibit-insurance, accessed July 24, 2020.

Abernathy, Ralph D., "Biography," kinginstitute.stanford.edu/encyclopedia/ abernathy-ralph-david, accessed May 27, 2020.

Adams, Brooke, "Joseph Paul Franklin timeline," archive.sltrib.com/article. php?id=57119474&itype=cmsid, accessed July 21, 2020.

"Affirmative Action," Brittanica, www.britannica.com/topic/ affirmative-action, accessed July 23, 2020.

Baker, Al, Goodman, David, and Mueller, Benjamin, "Beyond the chokehold: The path to Eric Garner's death," www.nytimes.com/2015/06/14/nyregion/ eric-garner-police-chokehold-staten-island.html, accessed 24 July 2020.

Barbour, Josephus Pius, Biography, kinginstitute.stanford.edu/encyclopedia/ barbour-josephus-pius, accessed August 27, 2020.

Blackburn, Bonnie, "Rev. Bill McGill: Speaking from a place of authenticity," www.fortwayne.com/people/rev-bill-mcgill/, accessed May 13, 2020.

"Boulder officer resigns following confrontation with Naropa University Student," denver.cbslocal.com/2019/05/16/zayd-atkinson-john-smyly- boulder-police-officer-resigns-naropa-university/, accessed July 26, 2020.

Bradner, Eric, "Obama: 'No sympathy' for violence in Ferguson," www.cnn. com/2014/11/25/politics/obama-holder-ferguson/index.html, accessed July 27, 2020.

Breu, Giovanna, "Trauma surgeon Jeff Towles saved Vernon Jordan 'The biggest wound I've ever seen,'" people.com/archive/trauma-surgeon- jeff-towles-saved-vernon-jordan-from-the-biggest-wound-ive-ever-seen- vol-14-no-4/, accessed May 28, 2020.

Brooks, Khristopher, "Redlining's legacy: Maps are gone, but the problem hasn't disappeared," www.cbsnews.com/news/redlining-what-is-history-mike-bloomberg-comments/, accessed July 24, 2020.

Brothers, Jr., Alfred, "The Fort Wayne Colored Giants," blog.history.in.gov/the-fort-wayne-colored-giants/, accessed August 8, 2020.

Buttram, Betty, "Walking down memory lane with a Selma marcher," *Fort Wayne Ink Spot*, www.fwinkspot.com/features/2018/7/28/walking-down-memory-road-with-a-selma-marcher, accessed May 29, 2020.

Carmody, Steve, and Winowiecki, Emma, "Before 'I have a Dream,' there was the 'Great Walk to Freedom,' In Detroit," www.michiganradio.org/post/i-have-dream-there-was-great-walk-freedom-detroit, accessed May 3, 2020

Chambers, Michelle, and Jehl, Russ, "A resolution initiating a process to request creation of a public display, commemorating Dr. Martin Luther King Jr's words and visit to Fort Wayne in 1963." Bill no. R-20-01-39, accessed April 14, 2020.

"Communism," kinginstitute.stanford.edu/encyclopedia/communism, accessed May 22, 2020.

"Dad, daughter, earn Doctor's degrees," *Muncie Star*, August 19, 1973, 11-A.

Daley, Jason, "The Unheralded Legacy of Civil Rights leader Dorothy Cotton," *Smithsonian*, www.smithsonianmag.com/smart-news/civil-rights-pioneer-dorothy-cotton-has-died-180969361/, accessed May 22, 2020.

Davis, Dominic-Madori, "One of the only four Black Fortune 500 CEO's just stepped down—here are the three that remain," *Business Insider*, www.businessinsider.com/there-are-four-black-fortune-500-ceos-here-they-are-2020-2, accessed July 22, 2020.

De La Beckwith, Byron, *Biography*, www.biography.com/crime-figure/byron-de-la-beckwith, accessed July 7, 2020.

Elejalde-Ruiz, Alexia, "Hiring bias study: Resumes with black, white, hispanic names treated the same," www.chicagotribune.com/business/ct-bias-hiring-0504-biz-20160503-story.html, accessed August 2, 2020.

Elliott, Debbie, "Rev. Fred Shuttlesworth, Civil Rights pioneer, dies," www.npr.org/2011/10/05/141083711/rev-fred-shuttlesworth-civil-rights-pioneer-dies, accessed September 19, 2020.

Fausset, Richard, "What we know about the shooting death of Ahmaud Arbery," www.nytimes.com/article/ahmaud-arbery-shooting-georgia.html, accessed July 24, 2020.

"Federal Bureau of Investigation (FBI)," kinginstitute.stanford.edu/encyclopedia/federal-bureau-investigation-fbi, accessed May 22, 2020.

"Fort Wayne official of NAACP Warned," *Muncie Evening Press*, October 10, 1963, p. 6.

"Fort Wayne, Indiana population: census 2010 and 2000 interactive map, demographics, statistics, quick facts," censusviewer.com/city/IN/Fort%20Wayne, accessed May 26, 2020.

Garrow, David, "The FBI and Martin Luther King," www.theatlantic. com/magazine/archive/2002/07/the-fbi-and-martin-luther-king/302537/, accessed July 9, 2020.

Gerdeman, Dina, "Minorities who 'whiten' job resumes get more interviews," hbswk.hbs.edu/item/minorities-who-whiten-job-resumes-get-more-interviews, accessed August 3, 2020.

Gstalter, Morgan, "Black Obama White House staffer has cops called on him while moving into new home," thehill.com/blogs/blog-briefing-room/news/385807-black-obama-white-house-staffer-has-cops-called-on-him-for, accessed August 16, 2020.

Guy, James Cameron, "Eugene Parker 1956–2016," www.blackpast.org/african-american-history/parker-eugene-1956-2016/, accessed July 23, 2020.

Hale, Rev. Phale, Biography, www.ohiostatehouse.org/museum/george-washington-williams-room/phale-d-hale-sr, accessed July 10, 2020.

Harter, Randy, "The Anthony Hotel *ca.* 1946." www.fortwaynereader.com/story.php?uid=3096, accessed June 29, 2020.

Have, Rev. Phale, Biography, www.dispatch.com/article/20090602/news/306029629, accessed July 10, 2020

"Herstory," blacklivesmatter.com/herstory/, accessed July 24, 2020

Hill, Evan, Tiefenthaler, Ainara, Triebert, Christiaan, Jordan, Drew, Willis, Haley, and Stein, Robin, "How George Floyd was killed in Police custody," www.nytimes.com/2020/05/31/us/george-floyd-investigation.html, accessed July 24, 2020.

Hissong, Rod, "Fort Wayne sports legend Eugene Parker dies," www.wane. com/news/fort-wayne-sports-legend-eugene-parker-dies/, accessed July 23, 2020.

"History of Union Baptist Church," www.genealogycenter.info/viewpage_ubcdirectory.php?realpage=35&display=Union_007, accessed July 1, 2020.

Holladay, Ruth, "Dr. Martin Luther King in Fort Wayne 1963," Blog, www. ruthholladay.com/2008/jan/21/dr-martin-luther-king-in-fort-wayne-1963/, accessed May 7, 2020.

Horton, Jake, "George Floyd: How far have African Americans come since the 1960s?" www.bbc.com/news/world-us-canada-52992795, accessed July 22, 2020.

"I shot Vernon Jordan, Franklin says," www.deseret.com/1996/4/8/19235463/i-shot-vernon-jordan-franklin-says, accessed May 28, 2020.

"I've been to the mountaintop," kinginstitute.stanford.edu/encyclopedia/ive-been-mountaintop, accessed July 15, 2020.

"Indiana Civil Rights Legislative History," www.in.gov/icrc/2350.htm, accessed May 13, 2020.

Jackson, Jimmie Lee, Biography, kinginstitute.stanford.edu/encyclopedia/jackson-jimmie-lee, accessed September 26, 2020.

"JFK televised address to the nation on Civil Rights," www.jfklibrary.org/learn/about-jfk/historic-speeches/televised-address-to-the-nation-on-civil-rights, accessed July 6, 2020.

Jones, Janelle, Schmitt, John, and Wilson, Valerie, "50 Years after the Kerner Commission," www.epi.org/publication/50-years-after-the-kerner-commission/, accessed July 22, 2020.

Jordan, Vernon E., Biography, www.britannica.com/biography/Vernon-E-Jordan-Jr, accessed July 20, 2020.

"Joseph Paul Franklin: a racist who admits it," www.upi.com/Archives/1982/08/18/Joseph-Paul-Franklin-A-racist-who-admits-it/6944398491200/, accessed July 21, 2020.

King III, Martin Luther, Biography, kinginstitute.stanford.edu/encyclopedia/king-martin-luther-iii, accessed May 27, 2020.

Lardner, Jr., George, "Vernon Jordan seriously injured by snipers bullet," www.washingtonpost.com/archive/politics/1980/05/30/vernon-jordan-seriously-injured-by-snipers-bullet/9556917d-b983-498e-82ee-7e11ea9f78ec/, accessed May 28, 2020.

Larson, Cindy, "Fort Wayne City Council takes first step in creating Martin Luther King Jr. display," www.fwbusiness.com/fwbusiness/article_2b92c45e-85c5-5ab5-a5d9-21bb45d9b54f.html, accessed April 20, 2020.

"Last night was not Fort Wayne," www.wane.com/news/local-news/last-night-was-not-fort-wayne-29-arrested-clean-up-underway/, accessed May 30, 2020.

Leininger, Kevin, "History's controversies can show progress—and so can the lack of controversy," www.news-sentinel.com/news/local-news/2020/01/28/kevin-leininger-historys-controversies-can-show-progress-and-so-can-the-lack-of-controversy/, accessed May 26, 2020; "Anthony's Tale," egen.fortwayne.com/ns/projects/history/scapes46.php, accessed April 17, 2020.

Levinson, Stanley, Biography, kinginstitute.stanford.edu/encyclopedia/levison-stanley-david, accessed June 8, 2020.

Lloyd, Natalie, Schamel, Wynell, and Potter, Lee Ann, "The 1963 March on Washington," www.socialstudies.org/sites/default/files/publications/se/6501/650103.html, accessed May 19, 2020.

"Longtime Pastor and Civil Rights leader has died," *News-Sentinel*, 27 February 2017, 1A.

Lopez, German, "Study: Anti-black hiring discrimination is as prevalent today as it was in 1989," www.vox.com/identities/2017/9/18/16307782/study-racism-jobs, accessed August 3, 2020.

Maranzani, Barbara, "King's Letter from Birmingham Jail: 50 Years Later," www.history.com/news/kings-letter-from-birmingham-jail-50-years-later, accessed May 27, 2020.

"March on Washington," openvault.wgbh.org/collections/march_on_washington/listening-guide, accessed June 15, 2020.

McLaughlin, Eliott, "Charlottesville rally violence: how we got here," www.cnn.com/2017/08/14/us/charlottesville-rally-timeline-tick-tock/index.html, accessed July 24, 2020.

McMaken, Corey, "1974: Explosive demolitions of Van Orman, Keenan Hotels," www.journalgazette.net/features/history-journal/20190725/in-1974-2-hotels-came-tumbling-down, accessed May 26, 2020.

Meroney, John, "What really happened between J. Edgar Hoover and MLK Jr.," www.theatlantic.com/entertainment/archive/2011/11/what-really-happened-between-j-edgar-hoover-and-mlk-jr/248319/, accessed July 29, 2020.

Morrison, Aaron, "In his final days, Ahmaud Arbery's life was at a crossroads," abcnews.go.com/US/wireStory/final-days-ahmaud-arberys-life-crossroads-70868985, accessed July 24, 2020.

"NAACP calls off protest at I & M in Fort Wayne," *Muncie Evening Press*, 21 September 1963, p. 7.

"NAACP History: Medgar Evers," www.naacp.org/naacp-history-medgar-evers/, accessed June 4, 2020.

"November 1963: Death of the President," www.jfklibrary.org/learn/about-jfk/jfk-in-history/november-22-1963-death-of-the-president, accessed July 9, 2020.

Odell, Hunter Pitts "Jack," Biography, kinginstitute.stanford.edu/encyclopedia/odell-hunter-pitts-jack, accessed July 7, 2020.

Perry, Imani, "Lorraine Hansberry, American radical: She pushed RFK to make a 'moral commitment' on Civil Rights," www.salon.com/2018/12/09/lorraine-hansberry-american-radical/, accessed May 13, 2020.

"Quick facts Fort Wayne, Indiana," www.census.gov/quickfacts/fact/table/fortwaynecityindiana/POP010210, accessed May 26, 2020.

"Remarks by President on Trayvon Martin," obamawhitehouse.archives.gov/the-press-office/2013/07/19/remarks-president-trayvon-martin, accessed July 27, 2020.

"Renowned football agent Eugene Parker dies at 60," www.foxsports.com/stories/nfl/renowned-football-agent-eugene-parker-dies-at-60, accessed July 23, 2020.

"Rev. Clyde Adams, local Pastor, Civil Rights leader, dies at 102," www.journalgazette.net/news/local/The-Rev--Clyde-Adams--local-pastor--civil-rights-leader--dies-at-102-18008305, accessed June 29, 2020.

Sakala, Leah, "Breaking down mass incarceration in the 2010 Census: State by State incarceration rates by race/ethnicity," www.prisonpolicy.org/reports/rates.html, accessed July 22, 2020.

Savage, Charlie, "When the culture wars hit Fort Wayne," www.politico.com/news/magazine/2020/07/31/culture-wars-fort-wayne-373011, accessed July 31, 2020.

Scott, Olive, "The legacy of Martin Luther King Jr's 1963 visit to Detroit," www.michiganradio.org/post/legacy-martin-luther-king-jr-s-1963-visit-detroit, accessed May 3, 2020.

Shapiro, Emily, "Key moments in Charleston church shooting case as Dylan Roof pleads guilty to state charges," abcnews.go.com/US/key-moments-charleston-church-shooting-case-dylann-roof/story?id=46701033, accessed July 24, 2020.

Somanader, Tanya, "President Obama delivers a statement on the Grand Jury decision in the death of Eric Garner," obamawhitehouse.archives.gov/blog/2014/12/03/president-obama-delivers-statement-grand-jury-decision-death-eric-garner, accessed July 27, 2020.

Speiser, Matthew, "This man roller skated 685 miles to attend Martin Luther King's 'I Have a Dream' speech," www.businessinsider.in/This-man-rollerskated-685-miles-to-attend-Martin-Luther-King-Jr-s-I-Have-A-Dream-speech/articleshow/48716221.cms, accessed June 4, 2020.

"Stand in the schoolhouse door," www.encyclopediaofalabama.org/article/h-1872, accessed July 6, 2020.

"Statement on the assassination of John F. Kennedy," kinginstitute.stanford.edu/king-papers/documents/statement-john-f-kennedy-assassination, accessed July 12, 2020.

Stephens, Lannyl, "The Baldwin-Kennedy meeting of 1963," gvshp.org/blog/2018/06/05/the-baldwin-kennedy-meeting-of-1963/, accessed May 13, 2020.

Thernstrom, Abigail and Stephan, "Black Progress: How far we've come, and how far we have to go," www.brookings.edu/articles/black-progress-how-far-weve-come-and-how-far-we-have-to-go/, accessed July 22, 2020

Thomas, Clarence, Biography, https://www.oyez.org/justices/clarence_thomas, accessed July 23, 2020.

Thornbrough, Emma Lou, "Breaking Racial Barriers to public accommodations in Indiana 1935 to 1963," *Indiana Magazine of History*, December 1987 Volume 83, Number 4, pp. 301-343.

"Timeline of events in shooting of Michael Brown in Ferguson," apnews.com/article/9aa32033692547699a3b61da8fd1fc62, accessed July 24, 2020.

"Trayvon Martin shooting fast facts," www.cnn.com/2013/06/05/us/trayvon-martin-shooting-fast-facts/index.html, accessed July 25, 2020.

Trescott, Jacqueline, "Vernon Jordan: battle scars," www.washingtonpost.com/archive/lifestyle/1980/10/27/vernon-jordan-battle-scars-38/8ed15369-6d99-4754-ae4e-dd14d90bb2cb/, accessed July 21, 2020.

Vera, Amir, "White woman who called police on black man bird watching in Central Park has been fired," www.cnn.com/2020/05/26/us/central-park-video-dog-video-african-american-trnd/index.html, accessed July 27, 2020.

"Wallace faces Indiana pickets," *The Wilmington Morning News*, 2 May 1964, p. 3.

"Wallace threatened by Fort Wayne 'bomb.'" *Indianapolis Star*, 2 May 1964, p. 1.

Webb, Jon, "Indiana still has a racism problem," www.courierpress.com/story/opinion/columnists/jon-webb/2017/11/07/webb-indiana-still-has-racism-problem/827560001/, accessed June 5, 2020.

Wertheim, Jon, "Remembering Eugene Parker, a rare agent who didn't seek the spotlight," www.si.com/nfl/2016/04/15/eugene-parker-nfl-agent-death, accessed July 23, 2020.

Wiley, Kelly, "Brunswick Attorney says he released deadly shooting video because people had right know," www.news4jax.com/news/georgia/2020/05/07/brunswick-attorney-says-he-released-deadly-shooting-video-because-people-had-right-to-know/, accessed September 28, 2020.

Wright-Edelman, Marian, "Remembering Fred Shuttlesworth: The most courageous man in America," www.childrensdefense.org/child-watch-columns/health/2011/remembering-fred-shuttlesworth-the-most-courageous-man-in-america/, accessed October 2, 2020.

Yan, Holly, "This is why everyday racial profiling is so dangerous," www.cnn.com/2018/05/11/us/everyday-racial-profiling-consequences-trnd/index.html, accessed July 24, 2020.

Print

"A dream left incomplete," editorial, *Journal-Gazette*, June 2, 2019, 9A.

"A lifetime ago, lessons learned in Indiana still carry Jordan today," editorial, *Journal-Gazette*, May 15, 2018, 8A.

"Allen County Photo Album 1960–1969," *News-Sentinel*, 2018

Antoine, Rick, and Fullam, Pete, "National Urban League Chief Vernon Jordan shot critically," *Journal-Gazette*, May 29, 1980, 1A.

"Article on King cited," letter to editor, *News-Sentinel*, May 21, 1963, 6A.

Bashore, Wesley, "Martin Luther King talks here May 28," *Journal-Gazette*, May 1, 1963, 1C; "We're confident of winning 'all freedoms:' King," *Journal-Gazette*, June 6, 1963, 1A; "King explains civil disobedience stand," *Journal-Gazette*, June 6, 1963, 1B; "Gov. Wallace continues attacks on Rights bill; fears 'take-over,'" *Journal-Gazette*, May 2, 1964, 1A; "Wallace's Civil Rights stand denounced by 250 pickets," *Journal-Gazette*, May 2, 1964, 1B; "Integration goal explained by Urban League director," *Journal-Gazette*, February 28, 1963.

"Carlin defends Martin Luther King," letter to editor, *News-Sentinel*, June 3, 1963, 6A.

Civil Rights Chronicle: The African American struggle for freedom. Publications International, 2003.

"Clergy back appearance of Dr. King," *Journal-Gazette*, May 27, 1963.

Cochrane, Bob, "NAACP eyes boycotting, picket use," *News-Sentinel*, September 25, 1963, p. 1E.

"Demonstrations in Fort Wayne pledged," *The Greenfield Daily Reporter*, June 13, 1963, p. 9.

Derringer, Alan, "Protests and Promises: A historical perspective of the Civil Rights struggle in Fort Wayne," *News-Sentinel*, February 7, 1995.

"Dr. Scott gets top school post," *News-Sentinel*, December 2, 1976, 1C.

Duffy, Jamie, "Delayed MLK III gives call to action," *Journal-Gazette*, June 6, 2019.

"Failure of program cited by Wilkerson," *Journal-Gazette*, May 24, 1963.

Ferguson, William, "King's memorial dignified by quiet, moving service," *News-Sentinel*, April 8, 1968, 1B.

"First Negro named to city school post," *News-Sentinel*, May 28, 1965, 1B.

"Fort Wayne Sympathy March participated in by hundreds," *News-Sentinel*, September 23, 1963, 1C.

"Frontiers Slate Midwest Parley," *News-Sentinel*, March 16, 1962, p. 21.

Graff, Jerry, "Ex-Klan member candidate," *News-Sentinel*, May 3, 1980, 3A; "Mayor: We inherited discrimination problems," *News-Sentinel*, April 10, 1979, 1C; "Nuckols calls city anti-bias plan inadequate," *News-Sentinel*, June 8, 1979, 1C; "Press questions Carter," *News-Sentinel*, June 2, 1980, 1A.

Guthrie, Thomas, and Richardson, Valerie, "A demographic profile of Allen County, Indiana," Community Research Institute, Indiana University-Purdue University Fort Wayne, 2003.

Harbison, Janet, "Anatomy of a Quantity-Quality," *Presbyterian Life*, January 1, 1966, pp. 10-16.

Harter, Randolph, and Leonard, Craig, *Legendary Locals of Fort Wayne* (Arcadia Publishing, 2015).

Helmke, Mark, "Klan's 'revival' demonstrates ineffectiveness," *News-Sentinel*, September 10, 1979, 1C; "Ku Klux Klan fights image problem," *News-Sentinel*, June 26, 1978, 1C; "Moses focuses on GOP Klansman," *News-Sentinel*, February 26, 1979, 1B.

"His Dream lives on," *News-Sentinel*, August 27, 2003, 1F.

History of Fort Wayne and Allen County, 1700–2005, Volume I, (M.T. Publishing Co., 2006).

Hughes, Langston, *Selected Poems of Langston Hughes* (Vintage Books, 1959).

Isenhour, Dick, "Nuckols cites Affirmative plan flaws," *News-Sentinel*, August 9, 1979, 1C.

"It Starts Today, August 2020," *Fort Wayne Magazine*, Fort Wayne Newspapers.

Jonason, Bob, "Hiring plan prompts argument," *News-Sentinel*, August 19, 1980, 1C.

Kilbane, Kevin, "1960s Civil Rights icons to attend Fort Wayne," *News-Sentinel*, March 22, 2018; "Equality in Fort Wayne: Understanding history," *News-Sentinel*, February 11, 2004; "Dr. King's visit to the city sparked energy," *News-Sentinel*, January 14, 2000, 1F; "King's words echo long after his 1963 Fort Wayne," *News-Sentinel*, January 15, 2001, 1A; "Community honors minister whose church has no walls," *News-Sentinel*, October 5, 1995, 1A.

King, Martin Luther, *Why we can't wait* (Penguin, 1964).

King, Rod, "Barnett talks here as pickets protest," *News-Sentinel*, March 18, 1963, 1A.

King, Shannon, "Subtle racism hindered social efforts local blacks," *News-Sentinel*, August 2, 1999, 7A.

"King," *The Atlantic*, Spring 2018.

"King's, aides loyalty questioned," letter to editor, *News-Sentinel*, May 23, 1963, 6A.

Leininger, Kevin, "Wisdom of trial in doubt," *News-Sentinel*, August 18, 1982, p. 1A; "The execution of Joseph Paul Franklin," *News-Sentinel*, November 19, 2013, p. 1A; "Jackson preaches, endorses boycott," *News-Sentinel*, December 6, 1982, p. 1B

Leininger, Kevin, and Graff, Jerry, "K-Mart asserts facts don't justify boycott," *News-Sentinel*, December 6, 1982.

Lesley, Van, "Dr. King welcomed by ovation, pickets," *News-Sentinel*, June 6, 1963, 1D.

Levinson, Cynthia, *We've got a job: The 1963 Birmingham Children's March* (Peachtree, 2012).

Little, Sharon, "Blacks issue ultimatum on school integration," *News-Sentinel*, June 24, 1969, 1A.

"Longtime pastor and Civil Rights leader has died," *News-Sentinel*, February 27, 2017, 1A.

"Luther King's talk postponed; reset for June 5," *News-Sentinel*, May 14, 1963, 1C.

Madison, James, and Sandweiss, Lee Ann, *Hoosiers and the American Story* (Indiana Historical Press, 2014).

"Martin Luther King talks in Fort Wayne," *South Bend Tribune*, June 6, 1963, 1A.

Miller, Dodie Marie, *African Americans in Fort Wayne: The First 200 years* (Arcadia Publishing, 2000).

Montgomery, Adrianne, "Educator who broke race barrier retiring," *News-Sentinel*, March 22, 1986, 3A.

"NAACP Youth picket Four variety stores," *News-Sentinel*, April 16, 1960, p. 2.

"Newest service club gets its charter; will serve Negroes," *News-Sentinel*, January 27, 1958, p. 13

"Nuckols seeks hiring practice probe," *News-Sentinel*, August 3, 1977, 1C.

Pages of Time: 1963: Nostalgia News Report (Seek Publishing).

"Preacher saves souls, opens doors," *News-Sentinel*, October 11, 1986, 1C.

"Restoring honor to King's vision: Weekend's marchers should embrace his entire agenda," editorial, *Journal-Gazette*, August 27, 2010, 15A.

"Rev. White demanded equality," editorial, *Journal-Gazette*, February 14, 2001.

Richardson, Terri, "Follow King's footsteps in the area," *Journal-Gazette*, April 3, 2018.

Seigel, Peggy, "Pushing the color line: Race and Employment in Fort Wayne, Indiana 1933–1963," *Indiana Magazine of History*, September 2008, pp. 241-276.

Shawgo, Ron, "Small, silent, and shut out: City's black population denied good jobs by entrenched system," *Journal-Gazette*, June 2, 2013, 1A; "Resistance hardens as opportunities grow," *Journal-Gazette*, June 3, 2013, 1A; "Threatening letters precede King visit," *Journal-Gazette*, June 4, 2013, 1A; "After half century, view of protestor unchanged," *Journal-Gazette*, June 5, 2013, 1A; "MLK nephew Derek King addresses violence, poverty: urges discipline, awareness, equality," *Journal-Gazette*, June 6, 2013, 1A.

Souder, Mark, "Hugh McCulloch and the origins of professional baseball," *Old Fort News*, Volume 82, Number 1, 2019.

Stoiber, Julie, "15 blacks to be honored for mark on community," *News-Sentinel*, May 9, 1987, p. 1C.

Sutton, Marie, *The A.G. Gaston Motel in Birmingham: A Civil Rights Landmark* (The History Press, 2014).

"The changing face of the threat," editorial, *Journal-Gazette*, December 2, 2015.

Thompson, Robert, "Wallace ignores protestors, asks vote to 'shake liberals,'" *News-Sentinel*, May 2, 1964, 1A.

Thornbrough, Emma Lou, *Indiana blacks in the 20th century* (Indiana University Press, 2001).

"Urban League luncheon told of need for more progress," *News-Sentinel*, May 27, 1966, 3A.

Williams, Ernest, "Dr. King explains Negro struggle," *News-Sentinel*, June 6, 1963, 1A; "JFK Rights actions falls short: King," *News-Sentinel*, June 6, 1963, 1D.

Videos

"John F. Kennedy's 1963 Televised address to the nation on Civil Rights," *YouTube*, uploaded by JFK Library, June 5, 2020, www.youtube.com/watch?v=58O2De-iPOk.

"Martin Luther King's last speech 'I've been to the mountaintop,'" *YouTube*, uploaded by NewsPoliticsInfo, April 4, 2010, www.youtube.com/watch?v=Oehry1JC9Rk.

"MLK III speaks in Fort Wayne," *YouTube*, uploaded by WANE-15, June 6, 2019, www.youtube.com/watch?v=tkf1YPqlrrM.

"Remembering Martin Luther King's famed 'I Have a Dream' speech," *YouTube*, uploaded by Inside Edition, January 14, 2018, www.youtube.com/watch?v=3P_s3ChZlRY.

"RFK speaks after MLK killed," *YouTube*, uploaded by History April 4, 2018, www.youtube.com/watch?v=_bDlET_gK68.

About the Author

CHRIS ELLIOTT is a lifelong Fort Wayne, Indiana resident who first developed an interest in Martin Luther King and a passion for the Civil Rights movement as a teenager. He still resides in Fort Wayne where he teaches high school history. Chris lives with his wife, Alicia, and son, Nathan. He is also the proud stepfather to three adult stepchildren, and one grandchild.